Much Ado About Nothing

By Edward de Vere

Art:
Portrait of Edward de Vere
17th Earl of Oxford (1550-1604)

This edition produced by
Verus Publishing

V | P

www.verusbooks.com

ISBN: 978-1-951267-37-7
Imprint / Publisher: Verus Publishing

The Author

Edward de Vere, 17th Earl of Oxford

Biography and Bibliography
After the Play

A Preverse

Drone on ye learned scholars of the day
As to with whom the words ahead the credit lay.
For our part though can be no further doubt
That the author of these words has been found out
To be a person lordly and refined
On whom the light of wit so boldly shined
That to keep this wit from tearing in the fray
He gave another, lesser wit his say.

Now let the least of wits
That writes these paltry lines
Yield to him whose peerless name
Should be with reverence spake.
Let this name be not of history's misassigns
Whose pen and verse have made the earth to shake.

Much Ado About Nothing

By Edward de Vere

The Main Characters

Benedick - A lord and soldier from Padua

Beatrice - Niece of Leonato

Hero - Daughter of Leonato

Don Pedro - Prince of Aragon

Don John - 'the Bastard Prince'- Brother of Don Pedro

Claudio - A Count of Florence

Leonato - Governor of Messina - Father of Hero

Antonio - Brother of Leonato

Balthasar - Attendant of Don Pedro

Borachio, Conrade - Followers of Don John

Margaret, Ursula - Attendants of Hero

Dogberry - The Constable in charge of The Watch

The Watch - Watchmen of Messina

Verges - The Headborough - Dogberry's partner
Friar Francis - A priest
A Sexton - The judge at the trial of Borachio
a Boy - Servant of Benedick

And now, the Play...

ACT I

SCENE I.

Before LEONATO'S house.

Enter LEONATO, HERO, and BEATRICE, with a Messenger

LEONATO

> I learn in this letter that Don Peter of Arragon
> comes this night to Messina.

Messenger

> He is very near by this: he was not three leagues off
> when I left him.

LEONATO

> How many gentlemen have you lost in this action?

Messenger

> But few of any sort, and none of name.

LEONATO

> A victory is twice itself when the achiever brings
> home full numbers. I find here that Don Peter hath
> bestowed much honour on a young Florentine called
> Claudio.

Messenger

> Much deserved on his part and equally remembered by
> Don Pedro: he hath borne himself beyond the
> promise of his age, doing, in the figure of a lamb,
> the feats of a lion: he hath indeed better
> bettered expectation than you must expect of me to
> tell you how.

LEONATO

> He hath an uncle here in Messina will be very much
> glad of it.

Messenger

> I have already delivered him letters, and there

6

appears much joy in him; even so much that joy could
not show itself modest enough without a badge of
bitterness.

LEONATO

Did he break out into tears?

Messenger

In great measure.

LEONATO

A kind overflow of kindness: there are no faces
truer than those that are so washed. How much
better is it to weep at joy than to joy at weeping!

BEATRICE

I pray you, is Signior Mountanto returned from the
wars or no?

Messenger

I know none of that name, lady: there was none such
in the army of any sort.

LEONATO

What is he that you ask for, niece?

HERO

My cousin means Signior Benedick of Padua.

Messenger

O, he's returned; and as pleasant as ever he was.

BEATRICE

He set up his bills here in Messina and challenged
Cupid at the flight; and my uncle's fool, reading
the challenge, subscribed for Cupid, and challenged
him at the bird-bolt. I pray you, how many hath he
killed and eaten in these wars? But how many hath
he killed? for indeed I promised to eat all of his killing.

LEONATO

Faith, niece, you tax Signior Benedick too much;
but he'll be meet with you, I doubt it not.

Messenger

He hath done good service, lady, in these wars.
BEATRICE
    You had musty victual, and he hath holp to eat it:
    he is a very valiant trencherman; he hath an
    excellent stomach.
Messenger
    And a good soldier too, lady.
BEATRICE
    And a good soldier to a lady: but what is he to a lord?
Messenger
    A lord to a lord, a man to a man; stuffed with all
    honourable virtues.
BEATRICE
    It is so, indeed; he is no less than a stuffed man:
    but for the stuffing,--well, we are all mortal.
LEONATO
    You must not, sir, mistake my niece. There is a
    kind of merry war betwixt Signior Benedick and her:
    they never meet but there's a skirmish of wit
    between them.
BEATRICE
    Alas! he gets nothing by that. In our last
    conflict four of his five wits went halting off, and
    now is the whole man governed with one: so that if
    he have wit enough to keep himself warm, let him
    bear it for a difference between himself and his
    horse; for it is all the wealth that he hath left,
    to be known a reasonable creature. Who is his
    companion now? He hath every month a new sworn
    brother.
Messenger
    Is't possible?
BEATRICE
    Very easily possible: he wears his faith but as

the fashion of his hat; it ever changes with the
next block.

Messenger

I see, lady, the gentleman is not in your books.

BEATRICE

No; an he were, I would burn my study. But, I pray
you, who is his companion? Is there no young
squarer now that will make a voyage with him to the
devil?

Messenger

He is most in the company of the right noble Claudio.

BEATRICE

O Lord, he will hang upon him like a disease: he
is sooner caught than the pestilence, and the taker
runs presently mad. God help the noble Claudio! if
he have caught the Benedick, it will cost him a
thousand pound ere a' be cured.

Messenger

I will hold friends with you, lady.

BEATRICE

Do, good friend.

LEONATO

You will never run mad, niece.

BEATRICE

No, not till a hot January.

Messenger

Don Pedro is approached.

*Enter DON PEDRO, DON JOHN, CLAUDIO, BENEDICK,
and BALTHASAR*

DON PEDRO

Good Signior Leonato, you are come to meet your
trouble: the fashion of the world is to avoid
cost, and you encounter it.

LEONATO

Never came trouble to my house in the likeness of
your grace: for trouble being gone, comfort should
remain; but when you depart from me, sorrow abides
and happiness takes his leave.

DON PEDRO

You embrace your charge too willingly. I think this
is your daughter.

LEONATO

Her mother hath many times told me so.

BENEDICK

Were you in doubt, sir, that you asked her?

LEONATO

Signior Benedick, no; for then were you a child.

DON PEDRO

You have it full, Benedick: we may guess by this
what you are, being a man Truly, the lady fathers
herself. Be happy, lady; for you are like an
honourable father.

BENEDICK

If Signior Leonato be her father, she would not
have his head on her shoulders for all Messina, as
like him as she is.

BEATRICE

I wonder that you will still be talking, Signior
Benedick: nobody marks you.

BENEDICK

What, my dear Lady Disdain! are you yet living?

BEATRICE

Is it possible disdain should die while she hath
such meet food to feed it as Signior Benedick?
Courtesy itself must convert to disdain, if you come
in her presence.

BENEDICK

Then is courtesy a turncoat. But it is certain I
am loved of all ladies, only you excepted: and I
would I could find in my heart that I had not a hard
heart; for, truly, I love none.

BEATRICE

A dear happiness to women: they would else have
been troubled with a pernicious suitor. I thank God
and my cold blood, I am of your humour for that: I
had rather hear my dog bark at a crow than a man
swear he loves me.

BENEDICK

God keep your ladyship still in that mind! so some
gentleman or other shall 'scape a predestinate
scratched face.

BEATRICE

Scratching could not make it worse, an 'twere such
a face as yours were.

BENEDICK

Well, you are a rare parrot-teacher.

BEATRICE

A bird of my tongue is better than a beast of yours.

BENEDICK

I would my horse had the speed of your tongue, and
so good a continuer. But keep your way, i' God's
name; I have done.

BEATRICE

You always end with a jade's trick: I know you of old.

DON PEDRO

That is the sum of all, Leonato. Signior Claudio
and Signior Benedick, my dear friend Leonato hath
invited you all. I tell him we shall stay here at
the least a month; and he heartily prays some
occasion may detain us longer. I dare swear he is no
hypocrite, but prays from his heart.

LEONATO

If you swear, my lord, you shall not be forsworn.

To DON JOHN

Let me bid you welcome, my lord: being reconciled to
the prince your brother, I owe you all duty.

DON JOHN

I thank you: I am not of many words, but I thank
you.

LEONATO

Please it your grace lead on?

DON PEDRO

Your hand, Leonato; we will go together.

Exeunt all except BENEDICK and CLAUDIO

CLAUDIO

Benedick, didst thou note the daughter of Signior
Leonato?

BENEDICK

I noted her not; but I looked on her.

CLAUDIO

Is she not a modest young lady?

BENEDICK

Do you question me, as an honest man should do, for
my simple true judgment; or would you have me speak
after my custom, as being a professed tyrant to their
sex?

CLAUDIO

No; I pray thee speak in sober judgment.

BENEDICK

Why, i' faith, methinks she's too low for a high
praise, too brown for a fair praise and too little
for a great praise: only this commendation I can

afford her, that were she other than she is, she
were unhandsome; and being no other but as she is, I
do not like her.

CLAUDIO

Thou thinkest I am in sport: I pray thee tell me
truly how thou likest her.

BENEDICK

Would you buy her, that you inquire after her?

CLAUDIO

Can the world buy such a jewel?

BENEDICK

Yea, and a case to put it into. But speak you this
with a sad brow? or do you play the flouting Jack,
to tell us Cupid is a good hare-finder and Vulcan a
rare carpenter? Come, in what key shall a man take
you, to go in the song?

CLAUDIO

In mine eye she is the sweetest lady that ever I
looked on.

BENEDICK

I can see yet without spectacles and I see no such
matter: there's her cousin, an she were not
possessed with a fury, exceeds her as much in beauty
as the first of May doth the last of December. But I
hope you have no intent to turn husband, have you?

CLAUDIO

I would scarce trust myself, though I had sworn the
contrary, if Hero would be my wife.

BENEDICK

Is't come to this? In faith, hath not the world
one man but he will wear his cap with suspicion?
Shall I never see a bachelor of three-score again?
Go to, i' faith; an thou wilt needs thrust thy neck
into a yoke, wear the print of it and sigh away

Sundays. Look Don Pedro is returned to seek you.

Re-enter DON PEDRO

DON PEDRO

What secret hath held you here, that you followed
not to Leonato's?

BENEDICK

I would your grace would constrain me to tell.

DON PEDRO

I charge thee on thy allegiance.

BENEDICK

You hear, Count Claudio: I can be secret as a dumb
man; I would have you think so; but, on my
allegiance, mark you this, on my allegiance. He is
in love. With who? now that is your grace's part.
Mark how short his answer is;--With Hero, Leonato's
short daughter.

CLAUDIO

If this were so, so were it uttered.

BENEDICK

Like the old tale, my lord: 'it is not so, nor
'twas not so, but, indeed, God forbid it should be
so.'

CLAUDIO

If my passion change not shortly, God forbid it
should be otherwise.

DON PEDRO

Amen, if you love her; for the lady is very well worthy.

CLAUDIO

You speak this to fetch me in, my lord.

DON PEDRO

By my troth, I speak my thought.

CLAUDIO

And, in faith, my lord, I spoke mine.

BENEDICK
And, by my two faiths and troths, my lord, I spoke
mine.
CLAUDIO
That I love her, I feel.
DON PEDRO
That she is worthy, I know.
BENEDICK
That I neither feel how she should be loved nor
know how she should be worthy, is the opinion that
fire cannot melt out of me: I will die in it at the stake.
DON PEDRO
Thou wast ever an obstinate heretic in the despite
of beauty.
CLAUDIO
And never could maintain his part but in the force
of his will.
BENEDICK
That a woman conceived me, I thank her; that she
brought me up, I likewise give her most humble
thanks: but that I will have a recheat winded in my
forehead, or hang my bugle in an invisible baldrick,
all women shall pardon me. Because I will not do
them the wrong to mistrust any, I will do myself the
right to trust none; and the fine is, for the which
I may go the finer, I will live a bachelor.
DON PEDRO
I shall see thee, ere I die, look pale with love.
BENEDICK
With anger, with sickness, or with hunger, my lord,
not with love: prove that ever I lose more blood
with love than I will get again with drinking, pick
out mine eyes with a ballad-maker's pen and hang me
up at the door of a brothel-house for the sign of

blind Cupid.

DON PEDRO

Well, if ever thou dost fall from this faith, thou
wilt prove a notable argument.

BENEDICK

If I do, hang me in a bottle like a cat and shoot
at me; and he that hits me, let him be clapped on
the shoulder, and called Adam.

DON PEDRO

Well, as time shall try: 'In time the savage bull
doth bear the yoke.'

BENEDICK

The savage bull may; but if ever the sensible
Benedick bear it, pluck off the bull's horns and set
them in my forehead: and let me be vilely painted,
and in such great letters as they write 'Here is
good horse to hire,' let them signify under my sign
'Here you may see Benedick the married man.'

CLAUDIO

If this should ever happen, thou wouldst be horn-mad.

DON PEDRO

Nay, if Cupid have not spent all his quiver in
Venice, thou wilt quake for this shortly.

BENEDICK

I look for an earthquake too, then.

DON PEDRO

Well, you temporize with the hours. In the
meantime, good Signior Benedick, repair to
Leonato's: commend me to him and tell him I will
not fail him at supper; for indeed he hath made
great preparation.

BENEDICK

I have almost matter enough in me for such an
embassage; and so I commit you--

CLAUDIO

To the tuition of God: From my house, if I had it,--
DON PEDRO

The sixth of July: Your loving friend, Benedick.
BENEDICK

Nay, mock not, mock not. The body of your
discourse is sometime guarded with fragments, and
the guards are but slightly basted on neither: ere
you flout old ends any further, examine your
conscience: and so I leave you.

Exit

CLAUDIO

My liege, your highness now may do me good.
DON PEDRO

My love is thine to teach: teach it but how,
And thou shalt see how apt it is to learn
Any hard lesson that may do thee good.
CLAUDIO

Hath Leonato any son, my lord?
DON PEDRO

No child but Hero; she's his only heir.
Dost thou affect her, Claudio?
CLAUDIO

O, my lord,
When you went onward on this ended action,
I look'd upon her with a soldier's eye,
That liked, but had a rougher task in hand
Than to drive liking to the name of love:
But now I am return'd and that war-thoughts
Have left their places vacant, in their rooms
Come thronging soft and delicate desires,
All prompting me how fair young Hero is,
Saying, I liked her ere I went to wars.

DON PEDRO

    Thou wilt be like a lover presently

    And tire the hearer with a book of words.

    If thou dost love fair Hero, cherish it,

    And I will break with her and with her father,

    And thou shalt have her. Was't not to this end

    That thou began'st to twist so fine a story?

CLAUDIO

    How sweetly you do minister to love,

    That know love's grief by his complexion!

    But lest my liking might too sudden seem,

    I would have salved it with a longer treatise.

DON PEDRO

    What need the bridge much broader than the flood?

    The fairest grant is the necessity.

    Look, what will serve is fit: 'tis once, thou lovest,

    And I will fit thee with the remedy.

    I know we shall have revelling to-night:

    I will assume thy part in some disguise

    And tell fair Hero I am Claudio,

    And in her bosom I'll unclasp my heart

    And take her hearing prisoner with the force

    And strong encounter of my amorous tale:

    Then after to her father will I break;

    And the conclusion is, she shall be thine.

    In practise let us put it presently.

Exeunt

SCENE II.

A room in LEONATO's house.

Enter LEONATO and ANTONIO, meeting

LEONATO

How now, brother! Where is my cousin, your son?
hath he provided this music?

ANTONIO

He is very busy about it. But, brother, I can tell
you strange news that you yet dreamt not of.

LEONATO

Are they good?

ANTONIO

As the event stamps them: but they have a good
cover; they show well outward. The prince and Count
Claudio, walking in a thick-pleached alley in mine
orchard, were thus much overheard by a man of mine:
the prince discovered to Claudio that he loved my
niece your daughter and meant to acknowledge it
this night in a dance: and if he found her
accordant, he meant to take the present time by the
top and instantly break with you of it.

LEONATO

Hath the fellow any wit that told you this?

ANTONIO

A good sharp fellow: I will send for him; and
question him yourself.

LEONATO

No, no; we will hold it as a dream till it appear
itself: but I will acquaint my daughter withal,
that she may be the better prepared for an answer,
if peradventure this be true. Go you and tell her of it.

Enter Attendants

Cousins, you know what you have to do. O, I cry you
mercy, friend; go you with me, and I will use your
skill. Good cousin, have a care this busy time.

Exeunt

SCENE III.

The same.

Enter DON JOHN and CONRADE

CONRADE

What the good-year, my lord! why are you thus out
of measure sad?

DON JOHN

There is no measure in the occasion that breeds;
therefore the sadness is without limit.

CONRADE

You should hear reason.

DON JOHN

And when I have heard it, what blessing brings it?

CONRADE

If not a present remedy, at least a patient
sufferance.

DON JOHN

I wonder that thou, being, as thou sayest thou art,
born under Saturn, goest about to apply a moral
medicine to a mortifying mischief. I cannot hide
what I am: I must be sad when I have cause and smile
at no man's jests, eat when I have stomach and wait
for no man's leisure, sleep when I am drowsy and
tend on no man's business, laugh when I am merry and
claw no man in his humour.

CONRADE

Yea, but you must not make the full show of this
till you may do it without controlment. You have of
late stood out against your brother, and he hath
ta'en you newly into his grace; where it is
impossible you should take true root but by the

fair weather that you make yourself: it is needful
that you frame the season for your own harvest.

DON JOHN

I had rather be a canker in a hedge than a rose in
his grace, and it better fits my blood to be
disdained of all than to fashion a carriage to rob
love from any: in this, though I cannot be said to
be a flattering honest man, it must not be denied
but I am a plain-dealing villain. I am trusted with
a muzzle and enfranchised with a clog; therefore I
have decreed not to sing in my cage. If I had my
mouth, I would bite; if I had my liberty, I would do
my liking: in the meantime let me be that I am and
seek not to alter me.

CONRADE

Can you make no use of your discontent?

DON JOHN

I make all use of it, for I use it only.
Who comes here?

Enter BORACHIO

What news, Borachio?

BORACHIO

I came yonder from a great supper: the prince your
brother is royally entertained by Leonato: and I
can give you intelligence of an intended marriage.

DON JOHN

Will it serve for any model to build mischief on?
What is he for a fool that betroths himself to
unquietness?

BORACHIO

Marry, it is your brother's right hand.

DON JOHN

Who? the most exquisite Claudio?

BORACHIO

Even he.

DON JOHN

A proper squire! And who, and who? which way looks he?

BORACHIO

Marry, on Hero, the daughter and heir of Leonato.

DON JOHN

A very forward March-chick! How came you to this?

BORACHIO

Being entertained for a perfumer, as I was smoking a musty room, comes me the prince and Claudio, hand in hand in sad conference: I whipt me behind the arras; and there heard it agreed upon that the prince should woo Hero for himself, and having obtained her, give her to Count Claudio.

DON JOHN

Come, come, let us thither: this may prove food to my displeasure. That young start-up hath all the glory of my overthrow: if I can cross him any way, I bless myself every way. You are both sure, and will assist me?

CONRADE

To the death, my lord.

DON JOHN

Let us to the great supper: their cheer is the greater that I am subdued. Would the cook were of my mind! Shall we go prove what's to be done?

BORACHIO

We'll wait upon your lordship.

Exeunt

ACT II

SCENE I.

A hall in LEONATO'S house.

Enter LEONATO, ANTONIO, HERO, BEATRICE, and
others

LEONATO
  Was not Count John here at supper?
ANTONIO
  I saw him not.
BEATRICE
  How tartly that gentleman looks! I never can see
  him but I am heart-burned an hour after.
HERO
  He is of a very melancholy disposition.
BEATRICE
  He were an excellent man that were made just in the
  midway between him and Benedick: the one is too
  like an image and says nothing, and the other too
  like my lady's eldest son, evermore tattling.
LEONATO
  Then half Signior Benedick's tongue in Count John's
  mouth, and half Count John's melancholy in Signior
  Benedick's face,--
BEATRICE
  With a good leg and a good foot, uncle, and money
  enough in his purse, such a man would win any woman
  in the world, if a' could get her good-will.
LEONATO
  By my troth, niece, thou wilt never get thee a
  husband, if thou be so shrewd of thy tongue.
ANTONIO

In faith, she's too curst.
BEATRICE
　　Too curst is more than curst: I shall lessen God's
　　sending that way; for it is said, 'God sends a curst
　　cow short horns;' but to a cow too curst he sends none.
LEONATO
　　So, by being too curst, God will send you no horns.
BEATRICE
　　Just, if he send me no husband; for the which
　　blessing I am at him upon my knees every morning and
　　evening. Lord, I could not endure a husband with a
　　beard on his face: I had rather lie in the woollen.
LEONATO
　　You may light on a husband that hath no beard.
BEATRICE
　　What should I do with him? dress him in my apparel
　　and make him my waiting-gentlewoman? He that hath a
　　beard is more than a youth, and he that hath no
　　beard is less than a man: and he that is more than
　　a youth is not for me, and he that is less than a
　　man, I am not for him: therefore, I will even take
　　sixpence in earnest of the bear-ward, and lead his
　　apes into hell.
LEONATO
　　Well, then, go you into hell?
BEATRICE
　　No, but to the gate; and there will the devil meet
　　me, like an old cuckold, with horns on his head, and
　　say 'Get you to heaven, Beatrice, get you to
　　heaven; here's no place for you maids:' so deliver
　　I up my apes, and away to Saint Peter for the
　　heavens; he shows me where the bachelors sit, and
　　there live we as merry as the day is long.
ANTONIO

[To HERO] Well, niece, I trust you will be ruled
by your father.
BEATRICE
Yes, faith; it is my cousin's duty to make curtsy
and say 'Father, as it please you.' But yet for all
that, cousin, let him be a handsome fellow, or else
make another curtsy and say 'Father, as it please
me.'
LEONATO
Well, niece, I hope to see you one day fitted with a
husband.
BEATRICE
Not till God make men of some other metal than
earth. Would it not grieve a woman to be
overmastered with a pierce of valiant dust? to make
an account of her life to a clod of wayward marl?
No, uncle, I'll none: Adam's sons are my brethren;
and, truly, I hold it a sin to match in my kindred.
LEONATO
Daughter, remember what I told you: if the prince
do solicit you in that kind, you know your answer.
BEATRICE
The fault will be in the music, cousin, if you be
not wooed in good time: if the prince be too
important, tell him there is measure in every thing
and so dance out the answer. For, hear me, Hero:
wooing, wedding, and repenting, is as a Scotch jig,
a measure, and a cinque pace: the first suit is hot
and hasty, like a Scotch jig, and full as
fantastical; the wedding, mannerly-modest, as a
measure, full of state and ancientry; and then comes
repentance and, with his bad legs, falls into the
cinque pace faster and faster, till he sink into his grave.
LEONATO

Cousin, you apprehend passing shrewdly.
BEATRICE
I have a good eye, uncle; I can see a church by daylight.
LEONATO
The revellers are entering, brother: make good room.

All put on their masks

Enter DON PEDRO, CLAUDIO, BENEDICK, BALTHASAR, DON JOHN, BORACHIO, MARGARET, URSULA and others, masked

DON PEDRO
Lady, will you walk about with your friend?
HERO
So you walk softly and look sweetly and say nothing,
I am yours for the walk; and especially when I walk
away.
DON PEDRO
With me in your company?
HERO
I may say so, when I please.
DON PEDRO
And when please you to say so?
HERO
When I like your favour; for God defend the lute
should be like the case!
DON PEDRO
My visor is Philemon's roof; within the house is Jove.
HERO
Why, then, your visor should be thatched.
DON PEDRO
Speak low, if you speak love.

Drawing her aside

BALTHASAR
Well, I would you did like me.
MARGARET
So would not I, for your own sake; for I have many ill-qualities.
BALTHASAR
Which is one?
MARGARET
I say my prayers aloud.
BALTHASAR
I love you the better: the hearers may cry, Amen.
MARGARET
God match me with a good dancer!
BALTHASAR
Amen.
MARGARET
And God keep him out of my sight when the dance is done! Answer, clerk.
BALTHASAR
No more words: the clerk is answered.
URSULA
I know you well enough; you are Signior Antonio.
ANTONIO
At a word, I am not.
URSULA
I know you by the waggling of your head.
ANTONIO
To tell you true, I counterfeit him.
URSULA
You could never do him so ill-well, unless you were the very man. Here's his dry hand up and down: you are he, you are he.
ANTONIO

At a word, I am not.
URSULA

Come, come, do you think I do not know you by your
excellent wit? can virtue hide itself? Go to,
mum, you are he: graces will appear, and there's an
end.
BEATRICE

Will you not tell me who told you so?
BENEDICK

No, you shall pardon me.
BEATRICE

Nor will you not tell me who you are?
BENEDICK

Not now.
BEATRICE

That I was disdainful, and that I had my good wit
out of the 'Hundred Merry Tales:'--well this was
Signior Benedick that said so.
BENEDICK

What's he?
BEATRICE

I am sure you know him well enough.
BENEDICK

Not I, believe me.
BEATRICE

Did he never make you laugh?
BENEDICK

I pray you, what is he?
BEATRICE

Why, he is the prince's jester: a very dull fool;
only his gift is in devising impossible slanders:
none but libertines delight in him; and the
commendation is not in his wit, but in his villany;
for he both pleases men and angers them, and then

they laugh at him and beat him. I am sure he is in
the fleet: I would he had boarded me.

BENEDICK

When I know the gentleman, I'll tell him what you say.

BEATRICE

Do, do: he'll but break a comparison or two on me;
which, peradventure not marked or not laughed at,
strikes him into melancholy; and then there's a
partridge wing saved, for the fool will eat no
supper that night.

Music

We must follow the leaders.

BENEDICK

In every good thing.

BEATRICE

Nay, if they lead to any ill, I will leave them at
the next turning.

*Dance. Then exeunt all except DON JOHN, BORACHIO,
and CLAUDIO*

DON JOHN

Sure my brother is amorous on Hero and hath
withdrawn her father to break with him about it.
The ladies follow her and but one visor remains.

BORACHIO

And that is Claudio: I know him by his bearing.

DON JOHN

Are not you Signior Benedick?

CLAUDIO

You know me well; I am he.

DON JOHN

Signior, you are very near my brother in his love:

he is enamoured on Hero; I pray you, dissuade him
from her: she is no equal for his birth: you may
do the part of an honest man in it.

CLAUDIO

How know you he loves her?

DON JOHN

I heard him swear his affection.

BORACHIO

So did I too; and he swore he would marry her to-night.

DON JOHN

Come, let us to the banquet.

Exeunt DON JOHN and BORACHIO

CLAUDIO

Thus answer I in the name of Benedick,
But hear these ill news with the ears of Claudio.
'Tis certain so; the prince wooes for himself.
Friendship is constant in all other things
Save in the office and affairs of love:
Therefore, all hearts in love use their own tongues;
Let every eye negotiate for itself
And trust no agent; for beauty is a witch
Against whose charms faith melteth into blood.
This is an accident of hourly proof,
Which I mistrusted not. Farewell, therefore, Hero!

Re-enter BENEDICK

BENEDICK

Count Claudio?

CLAUDIO

Yea, the same.

BENEDICK

Come, will you go with me?

CLAUDIO

Whither?

BENEDICK

Even to the next willow, about your own business,
county. What fashion will you wear the garland of?
about your neck, like an usurer's chain? or under
your arm, like a lieutenant's scarf? You must wear
it one way, for the prince hath got your Hero.

CLAUDIO

I wish him joy of her.

BENEDICK

Why, that's spoken like an honest drovier: so they
sell bullocks. But did you think the prince would
have served you thus?

CLAUDIO

I pray you, leave me.

BENEDICK

Ho! now you strike like the blind man: 'twas the
boy that stole your meat, and you'll beat the post.

CLAUDIO

If it will not be, I'll leave you.

Exit

BENEDICK

Alas, poor hurt fowl! now will he creep into sedges.
But that my Lady Beatrice should know me, and not
know me! The prince's fool! Ha? It may be I go
under that title because I am merry. Yea, but so I
am apt to do myself wrong; I am not so reputed: it
is the base, though bitter, disposition of Beatrice
that puts the world into her person and so gives me
out. Well, I'll be revenged as I may.

Re-enter DON PEDRO

DON PEDRO

Now, signior, where's the count? did you see him?

BENEDICK

Troth, my lord, I have played the part of Lady Fame.
I found him here as melancholy as a lodge in a
warren: I told him, and I think I told him true,
that your grace had got the good will of this young
lady; and I offered him my company to a willow-tree,
either to make him a garland, as being forsaken, or
to bind him up a rod, as being worthy to be whipped.

DON PEDRO

To be whipped! What's his fault?

BENEDICK

The flat transgression of a schoolboy, who, being
overjoyed with finding a birds' nest, shows it his
companion, and he steals it.

DON PEDRO

Wilt thou make a trust a transgression? The
transgression is in the stealer.

BENEDICK

Yet it had not been amiss the rod had been made,
and the garland too; for the garland he might have
worn himself, and the rod he might have bestowed on
you, who, as I take it, have stolen his birds' nest.

DON PEDRO

I will but teach them to sing, and restore them to
the owner.

BENEDICK

If their singing answer your saying, by my faith,
you say honestly.

DON PEDRO

The Lady Beatrice hath a quarrel to you: the
gentleman that danced with her told her she is much

wronged by you.

BENEDICK

O, she misused me past the endurance of a block!
an oak but with one green leaf on it would have
answered her; my very visor began to assume life and
scold with her. She told me, not thinking I had been
myself, that I was the prince's jester, that I was
duller than a great thaw; huddling jest upon jest
with such impossible conveyance upon me that I stood
like a man at a mark, with a whole army shooting at
me. She speaks poniards, and every word stabs:
if her breath were as terrible as her terminations,
there were no living near her; she would infect to
the north star. I would not marry her, though she
were endowed with all that Adam bad left him before
he transgressed: she would have made Hercules have
turned spit, yea, and have cleft his club to make
the fire too. Come, talk not of her: you shall find
her the infernal Ate in good apparel. I would to God
some scholar would conjure her; for certainly, while
she is here, a man may live as quiet in hell as in a
sanctuary; and people sin upon purpose, because they
would go thither; so, indeed, all disquiet, horror
and perturbation follows her.

DON PEDRO

Look, here she comes.

Enter CLAUDIO, BEATRICE, HERO, and LEONATO

BENEDICK

Will your grace command me any service to the
world's end? I will go on the slightest errand now
to the Antipodes that you can devise to send me on;
I will fetch you a tooth-picker now from the
furthest inch of Asia, bring you the length of

Prester John's foot, fetch you a hair off the great
Cham's beard, do you any embassage to the Pigmies,
rather than hold three words' conference with this
harpy. You have no employment for me?

DON PEDRO

None, but to desire your good company.

BENEDICK

O God, sir, here's a dish I love not: I cannot
endure my Lady Tongue.

Exit

DON PEDRO

Come, lady, come; you have lost the heart of
Signior Benedick.

BEATRICE

Indeed, my lord, he lent it me awhile; and I gave
him use for it, a double heart for his single one:
marry, once before he won it of me with false dice,
therefore your grace may well say I have lost it.

DON PEDRO

You have put him down, lady, you have put him down.

BEATRICE

So I would not he should do me, my lord, lest I
should prove the mother of fools. I have brought
Count Claudio, whom you sent me to seek.

DON PEDRO

Why, how now, count! wherefore are you sad?

CLAUDIO

Not sad, my lord.

DON PEDRO

How then? sick?

CLAUDIO

Neither, my lord.

BEATRICE

The count is neither sad, nor sick, nor merry, nor
well; but civil count, civil as an orange, and
something of that jealous complexion.

DON PEDRO

I' faith, lady, I think your blazon to be true;
though, I'll be sworn, if he be so, his conceit is
false. Here, Claudio, I have wooed in thy name, and
fair Hero is won: I have broke with her father,
and his good will obtained: name the day of
marriage, and God give thee joy!

LEONATO

Count, take of me my daughter, and with her my
fortunes: his grace hath made the match, and an
grace say Amen to it.

BEATRICE

Speak, count, 'tis your cue.

CLAUDIO

Silence is the perfectest herald of joy: I were
but little happy, if I could say how much. Lady, as
you are mine, I am yours: I give away myself for
you and dote upon the exchange.

BEATRICE

Speak, cousin; or, if you cannot, stop his mouth
with a kiss, and let not him speak neither.

DON PEDRO

In faith, lady, you have a merry heart.

BEATRICE

Yea, my lord; I thank it, poor fool, it keeps on
the windy side of care. My cousin tells him in his
ear that he is in her heart.

CLAUDIO

And so she doth, cousin.

BEATRICE

Good Lord, for alliance! Thus goes every one to the

world but I, and I am sunburnt; I may sit in a
corner and cry heigh-ho for a husband!

DON PEDRO

Lady Beatrice, I will get you one.

BEATRICE

I would rather have one of your father's getting.
Hath your grace ne'er a brother like you? Your
father got excellent husbands, if a maid could come by
them.

DON PEDRO

Will you have me, lady?

BEATRICE

No, my lord, unless I might have another for
working-days: your grace is too costly to wear
every day. But, I beseech your grace, pardon me: I
was born to speak all mirth and no matter.

DON PEDRO

Your silence most offends me, and to be merry best
becomes you; for, out of question, you were born in
a merry hour.

BEATRICE

No, sure, my lord, my mother cried; but then there
was a star danced, and under that was I born.
Cousins, God give you joy!

LEONATO

Niece, will you look to those things I told you of?

BEATRICE

I cry you mercy, uncle. By your grace's pardon.

Exit

DON PEDRO

By my troth, a pleasant-spirited lady.

LEONATO

There's little of the melancholy element in her, my

lord: she is never sad but when she sleeps, and
not ever sad then; for I have heard my daughter say,
she hath often dreamed of unhappiness and waked
herself with laughing.

DON PEDRO

She cannot endure to hear tell of a husband.

LEONATO

O, by no means: she mocks all her wooers out of suit.

DON PEDRO

She were an excellent wife for Benedict.

LEONATO

O Lord, my lord, if they were but a week married,
they would talk themselves mad.

DON PEDRO

County Claudio, when mean you to go to church?

CLAUDIO

To-morrow, my lord: time goes on crutches till love
have all his rites.

LEONATO

Not till Monday, my dear son, which is hence a just
seven-night; and a time too brief, too, to have all
things answer my mind.

DON PEDRO

Come, you shake the head at so long a breathing:
but, I warrant thee, Claudio, the time shall not go
dully by us. I will in the interim undertake one of
Hercules' labours; which is, to bring Signior
Benedick and the Lady Beatrice into a mountain of
affection the one with the other. I would fain have
it a match, and I doubt not but to fashion it, if
you three will but minister such assistance as I
shall give you direction.

LEONATO

My lord, I am for you, though it cost me ten

nights' watchings.

CLAUDIO

And I, my lord.

DON PEDRO

And you too, gentle Hero?

HERO

I will do any modest office, my lord, to help my cousin to a good husband.

DON PEDRO

And Benedick is not the unhopefullest husband that I know. Thus far can I praise him; he is of a noble strain, of approved valour and confirmed honesty. I will teach you how to humour your cousin, that she shall fall in love with Benedick; and I, with your two helps, will so practise on Benedick that, in despite of his quick wit and his queasy stomach, he shall fall in love with Beatrice. If we can do this, Cupid is no longer an archer: his glory shall be ours, for we are the only love-gods. Go in with me, and I will tell you my drift.

Exeunt

SCENE II.

The same.

Enter DON JOHN and BORACHIO

DON JOHN

It is so; the Count Claudio shall marry the daughter of Leonato.

BORACHIO

Yea, my lord; but I can cross it.

DON JOHN

Any bar, any cross, any impediment will be

medicinable to me: I am sick in displeasure to him,
and whatsoever comes athwart his affection ranges
evenly with mine. How canst thou cross this marriage?
BORACHIO
Not honestly, my lord; but so covertly that no
dishonesty shall appear in me.
DON JOHN
Show me briefly how.
BORACHIO
I think I told your lordship a year since, how much
I am in the favour of Margaret, the waiting
gentlewoman to Hero.
DON JOHN
I remember.
BORACHIO
I can, at any unseasonable instant of the night,
appoint her to look out at her lady's chamber window.
DON JOHN
What life is in that, to be the death of this marriage?
BORACHIO
The poison of that lies in you to temper. Go you to
the prince your brother; spare not to tell him that
he hath wronged his honour in marrying the renowned
Claudio--whose estimation do you mightily hold
up--to a contaminated stale, such a one as Hero.
DON JOHN
What proof shall I make of that?
BORACHIO
Proof enough to misuse the prince, to vex Claudio,
to undo Hero and kill Leonato. Look you for any
other issue?
DON JOHN
Only to despite them, I will endeavour any thing.
BORACHIO

Go, then; find me a meet hour to draw Don Pedro and the Count Claudio alone: tell them that you know that Hero loves me; intend a kind of zeal both to the prince and Claudio, as,--in love of your brother's honour, who hath made this match, and his friend's reputation, who is thus like to be cozened with the semblance of a maid,--that you have discovered thus. They will scarcely believe this without trial: offer them instances; which shall bear no less likelihood than to see me at her chamber-window, hear me call Margaret Hero, hear Margaret term me Claudio; and bring them to see this the very night before the intended wedding,--for in the meantime I will so fashion the matter that Hero shall be absent,--and there shall appear such seeming truth of Hero's disloyalty that jealousy shall be called assurance and all the preparation overthrown.

DON JOHN

Grow this to what adverse issue it can, I will put it in practise. Be cunning in the working this, and thy fee is a thousand ducats.

BORACHIO

Be you constant in the accusation, and my cunning shall not shame me.

DON JOHN

I will presently go learn their day of marriage.

Exeunt

SCENE III.

LEONATO'S orchard.

Enter BENEDICK

BENEDICK
  Boy!

Enter Boy

Boy
  Signior?
BENEDICK
  In my chamber-window lies a book: bring it hither
  to me in the orchard.
Boy
  I am here already, sir.
BENEDICK
  I know that; but I would have thee hence, and here
  again.

Exit Boy

I do much wonder that one man, seeing how much
another man is a fool when he dedicates his
behaviors to love, will, after he hath laughed at
such shallow follies in others, become the argument
of his own scorn by failing in love: and such a man
is Claudio. I have known when there was no music
with him but the drum and the fife; and now had he
rather hear the tabour and the pipe: I have known
when he would have walked ten mile a-foot to see a
good armour; and now will he lie ten nights awake,
carving the fashion of a new doublet. He was wont to
speak plain and to the purpose, like an honest man
and a soldier; and now is he turned orthography; his

words are a very fantastical banquet, just so many
strange dishes. May I be so converted and see with
these eyes? I cannot tell; I think not: I will not
be sworn, but love may transform me to an oyster; but
I'll take my oath on it, till he have made an oyster
of me, he shall never make me such a fool. One woman
is fair, yet I am well; another is wise, yet I am
well; another virtuous, yet I am well; but till all
graces be in one woman, one woman shall not come in
my grace. Rich she shall be, that's certain; wise,
or I'll none; virtuous, or I'll never cheapen her;
fair, or I'll never look on her; mild, or come not
near me; noble, or not I for an angel; of good
discourse, an excellent musician, and her hair shall
be of what colour it please God. Ha! the prince and
Monsieur Love! I will hide me in the arbour.

Withdraws

Enter DON PEDRO, CLAUDIO, and LEONATO

DON PEDRO
  Come, shall we hear this music?
CLAUDIO
  Yea, my good lord. How still the evening is,
  As hush'd on purpose to grace harmony!
DON PEDRO
  See you where Benedick hath hid himself?
CLAUDIO
  O, very well, my lord: the music ended,
  We'll fit the kid-fox with a pennyworth.

Enter BALTHASAR with Music

DON PEDRO

Come, Balthasar, we'll hear that song again.

BALTHASAR

O, good my lord, tax not so bad a voice
To slander music any more than once.

DON PEDRO

It is the witness still of excellency
To put a strange face on his own perfection.
I pray thee, sing, and let me woo no more.

BALTHASAR

Because you talk of wooing, I will sing;
Since many a wooer doth commence his suit
To her he thinks not worthy, yet he wooes,
Yet will he swear he loves.

DON PEDRO

Now, pray thee, come;
Or, if thou wilt hold longer argument,
Do it in notes.

BALTHASAR

Note this before my notes;
There's not a note of mine that's worth the noting.

DON PEDRO

Why, these are very crotchets that he speaks;
Note, notes, forsooth, and nothing.

Air

BENEDICK

Now, divine air! now is his soul ravished! Is it
not strange that sheeps' guts should hale souls out
of men's bodies? Well, a horn for my money, when
all's done.

The Song

BALTHASAR

43

Sigh no more, ladies, sigh no more,
Men were deceivers ever,
One foot in sea and one on shore,
To one thing constant never:
Then sigh not so, but let them go,
And be you blithe and bonny,
Converting all your sounds of woe
Into Hey nonny, nonny.
Sing no more ditties, sing no moe,
Of dumps so dull and heavy;
The fraud of men was ever so,
Since summer first was leafy:
Then sigh not so, & c.

DON PEDRO

By my troth, a good song.

BALTHASAR

And an ill singer, my lord.

DON PEDRO

Ha, no, no, faith; thou singest well enough for a shift.

BENEDICK

An he had been a dog that should have howled thus,
they would have hanged him: and I pray God his bad
voice bode no mischief. I had as lief have heard the
night-raven, come what plague could have come after
it.

DON PEDRO

Yea, marry, dost thou hear, Balthasar? I pray thee,
get us some excellent music; for to-morrow night we
would have it at the Lady Hero's chamber-window.

BALTHASAR

The best I can, my lord.

DON PEDRO

Do so: farewell.

Exit BALTHASAR

44

Come hither, Leonato. What was it you told me of
to-day, that your niece Beatrice was in love with
Signior Benedick?

CLAUDIO

O, ay: stalk on. stalk on; the fowl sits. I did
never think that lady would have loved any man.

LEONATO

No, nor I neither; but most wonderful that she
should so dote on Signior Benedick, whom she hath in
all outward behaviors seemed ever to abhor.

BENEDICK

Is't possible? Sits the wind in that corner?

LEONATO

By my troth, my lord, I cannot tell what to think
of it but that she loves him with an enraged
affection: it is past the infinite of thought.

DON PEDRO

May be she doth but counterfeit.

CLAUDIO

Faith, like enough.

LEONATO

O God, counterfeit! There was never counterfeit of
passion came so near the life of passion as she
discovers it.

DON PEDRO

Why, what effects of passion shows she?

CLAUDIO

Bait the hook well; this fish will bite.

LEONATO

What effects, my lord? She will sit you, you heard
my daughter tell you how.

CLAUDIO

She did, indeed.

DON PEDRO

How, how, pray you? You amaze me: I would have I
thought her spirit had been invincible against all
assaults of affection.

LEONATO

I would have sworn it had, my lord; especially
against Benedick.

BENEDICK

I should think this a gull, but that the
white-bearded fellow speaks it: knavery cannot,
sure, hide himself in such reverence.

CLAUDIO

He hath ta'en the infection: hold it up.

DON PEDRO

Hath she made her affection known to Benedick?

LEONATO

No; and swears she never will: that's her torment.

CLAUDIO

'Tis true, indeed; so your daughter says: 'Shall
I,' says she, 'that have so oft encountered him
with scorn, write to him that I love him?'

LEONATO

This says she now when she is beginning to write to
him; for she'll be up twenty times a night, and
there will she sit in her smock till she have writ a
sheet of paper: my daughter tells us all.

CLAUDIO

Now you talk of a sheet of paper, I remember a
pretty jest your daughter told us of.

LEONATO

O, when she had writ it and was reading it over, she
found Benedick and Beatrice between the sheet?

CLAUDIO

That.

LEONATO

O, she tore the letter into a thousand halfpence;
railed at herself, that she should be so immodest
to write to one that she knew would flout her; 'I
measure him,' says she, 'by my own spirit; for I
should flout him, if he writ to me; yea, though I
love him, I should.'

CLAUDIO

Then down upon her knees she falls, weeps, sobs,
beats her heart, tears her hair, prays, curses; 'O
sweet Benedick! God give me patience!'

LEONATO

She doth indeed; my daughter says so: and the
ecstasy hath so much overborne her that my daughter
is sometime afeared she will do a desperate outrage
to herself: it is very true.

DON PEDRO

It were good that Benedick knew of it by some
other, if she will not discover it.

CLAUDIO

To what end? He would make but a sport of it and
torment the poor lady worse.

DON PEDRO

An he should, it were an alms to hang him. She's an
excellent sweet lady; and, out of all suspicion,
she is virtuous.

CLAUDIO

And she is exceeding wise.

DON PEDRO

In every thing but in loving Benedick.

LEONATO

O, my lord, wisdom and blood combating in so tender
a body, we have ten proofs to one that blood hath
the victory. I am sorry for her, as I have just

cause, being her uncle and her guardian.

DON PEDRO

I would she had bestowed this dotage on me: I would
have daffed all other respects and made her half
myself. I pray you, tell Benedick of it, and hear
what a' will say.

LEONATO

Were it good, think you?

CLAUDIO

Hero thinks surely she will die; for she says she
will die, if he love her not, and she will die, ere
she make her love known, and she will die, if he woo
her, rather than she will bate one breath of her
accustomed crossness.

DON PEDRO

She doth well: if she should make tender of her
love, 'tis very possible he'll scorn it; for the
man, as you know all, hath a contemptible spirit.

CLAUDIO

He is a very proper man.

DON PEDRO

He hath indeed a good outward happiness.

CLAUDIO

Before God! and, in my mind, very wise.

DON PEDRO

He doth indeed show some sparks that are like wit.

CLAUDIO

And I take him to be valiant.

DON PEDRO

As Hector, I assure you: and in the managing of
quarrels you may say he is wise; for either he
avoids them with great discretion, or undertakes
them with a most Christian-like fear.

LEONATO

If he do fear God, a' must necessarily keep peace:
if he break the peace, he ought to enter into a
quarrel with fear and trembling.

DON PEDRO

And so will he do; for the man doth fear God,
howsoever it seems not in him by some large jests
he will make. Well I am sorry for your niece. Shall
we go seek Benedick, and tell him of her love?

CLAUDIO

Never tell him, my lord: let her wear it out with
good counsel.

LEONATO

Nay, that's impossible: she may wear her heart out first.

DON PEDRO

Well, we will hear further of it by your daughter:
let it cool the while. I love Benedick well; and I
could wish he would modestly examine himself, to see
how much he is unworthy so good a lady.

LEONATO

My lord, will you walk? dinner is ready.

CLAUDIO

If he do not dote on her upon this, I will never
trust my expectation.

DON PEDRO

Let there be the same net spread for her; and that
must your daughter and her gentlewomen carry. The
sport will be, when they hold one an opinion of
another's dotage, and no such matter: that's the
scene that I would see, which will be merely a
dumb-show. Let us send her to call him in to dinner.

Exeunt DON PEDRO, CLAUDIO, and LEONATO

BENEDICK

[Coming forward] This can be no trick: the

conference was sadly borne. They have the truth of
this from Hero. They seem to pity the lady: it
seems her affections have their full bent. Love me!
why, it must be requited. I hear how I am censured:
they say I will bear myself proudly, if I perceive
the love come from her; they say too that she will
rather die than give any sign of affection. I did
never think to marry: I must not seem proud: happy
are they that hear their detractions and can put
them to mending. They say the lady is fair; 'tis a
truth, I can bear them witness; and virtuous; 'tis
so, I cannot reprove it; and wise, but for loving
me; by my troth, it is no addition to her wit, nor
no great argument of her folly, for I will be
horribly in love with her. I may chance have some
odd quirks and remnants of wit broken on me,
because I have railed so long against marriage: but
doth not the appetite alter? a man loves the meat
in his youth that he cannot endure in his age.
Shall quips and sentences and these paper bullets of
the brain awe a man from the career of his humour?
No, the world must be peopled. When I said I would
die a bachelor, I did not think I should live till I
were married. Here comes Beatrice. By this day!
she's a fair lady: I do spy some marks of love in
her.

Enter BEATRICE

BEATRICE
    Against my will I am sent to bid you come in to dinner.
BENEDICK
    Fair Beatrice, I thank you for your pains.
BEATRICE
    I took no more pains for those thanks than you take

pains to thank me: if it had been painful, I would
not have come.

BENEDICK

You take pleasure then in the message?

BEATRICE

Yea, just so much as you may take upon a knife's
point and choke a daw withal. You have no stomach,
signior: fare you well.

Exit

BENEDICK

Ha! 'Against my will I am sent to bid you come in
to dinner;' there's a double meaning in that 'I took
no more pains for those thanks than you took pains
to thank me.' that's as much as to say, Any pains
that I take for you is as easy as thanks. If I do
not take pity of her, I am a villain; if I do not
love her, I am a Jew. I will go get her picture.

Exit

ACT III

SCENE I.

LEONATO'S garden.

Enter HERO, MARGARET, and URSULA

HERO

Good Margaret, run thee to the parlor;
There shalt thou find my cousin Beatrice
Proposing with the prince and Claudio:
Whisper her ear and tell her, I and Ursula
Walk in the orchard and our whole discourse
Is all of her; say that thou overheard'st us;
And bid her steal into the pleached bower,
Where honeysuckles, ripen'd by the sun,
Forbid the sun to enter, like favourites,
Made proud by princes, that advance their pride
Against that power that bred it: there will she hide her,
To listen our purpose. This is thy office;
Bear thee well in it and leave us alone.

MARGARET

I'll make her come, I warrant you, presently.

Exit

HERO

Now, Ursula, when Beatrice doth come,
As we do trace this alley up and down,
Our talk must only be of Benedick.
When I do name him, let it be thy part
To praise him more than ever man did merit:
My talk to thee must be how Benedick
Is sick in love with Beatrice. Of this matter

Is little Cupid's crafty arrow made,
That only wounds by hearsay.

Enter BEATRICE, behind

Now begin;
For look where Beatrice, like a lapwing, runs
Close by the ground, to hear our conference.
URSULA
The pleasant'st angling is to see the fish
Cut with her golden oars the silver stream,
And greedily devour the treacherous bait:
So angle we for Beatrice; who even now
Is couched in the woodbine coverture.
Fear you not my part of the dialogue.
HERO
Then go we near her, that her ear lose nothing
Of the false sweet bait that we lay for it.

Approaching the bower

No, truly, Ursula, she is too disdainful;
I know her spirits are as coy and wild
As haggerds of the rock.
URSULA
But are you sure
That Benedick loves Beatrice so entirely?
HERO
So says the prince and my new-trothed lord.
URSULA
And did they bid you tell her of it, madam?
HERO
They did entreat me to acquaint her of it;
But I persuaded them, if they loved Benedick,
To wish him wrestle with affection,

And never to let Beatrice know of it.

URSULA

Why did you so? Doth not the gentleman
Deserve as full as fortunate a bed
As ever Beatrice shall couch upon?

HERO

O god of love! I know he doth deserve
As much as may be yielded to a man:
But Nature never framed a woman's heart
Of prouder stuff than that of Beatrice;
Disdain and scorn ride sparkling in her eyes,
Misprising what they look on, and her wit
Values itself so highly that to her
All matter else seems weak: she cannot love,
Nor take no shape nor project of affection,
She is so self-endeared.

URSULA

Sure, I think so;
And therefore certainly it were not good
She knew his love, lest she make sport at it.

HERO

Why, you speak truth. I never yet saw man,
How wise, how noble, young, how rarely featured,
But she would spell him backward: if fair-faced,
She would swear the gentleman should be her sister;
If black, why, Nature, drawing of an antique,
Made a foul blot; if tall, a lance ill-headed;
If low, an agate very vilely cut;
If speaking, why, a vane blown with all winds;
If silent, why, a block moved with none.
So turns she every man the wrong side out
And never gives to truth and virtue that
Which simpleness and merit purchaseth.

URSULA

Sure, sure, such carping is not commendable.

HERO

No, not to be so odd and from all fashions
As Beatrice is, cannot be commendable:
But who dare tell her so? If I should speak,
She would mock me into air; O, she would laugh me
Out of myself, press me to death with wit.
Therefore let Benedick, like cover'd fire,
Consume away in sighs, waste inwardly:
It were a better death than die with mocks,
Which is as bad as die with tickling.

URSULA

Yet tell her of it: hear what she will say.

HERO

No; rather I will go to Benedick
And counsel him to fight against his passion.
And, truly, I'll devise some honest slanders
To stain my cousin with: one doth not know
How much an ill word may empoison liking.

URSULA

O, do not do your cousin such a wrong.
She cannot be so much without true judgment--
Having so swift and excellent a wit
As she is prized to have--as to refuse
So rare a gentleman as Signior Benedick.

HERO

He is the only man of Italy.
Always excepted my dear Claudio.

URSULA

I pray you, be not angry with me, madam,
Speaking my fancy: Signior Benedick,
For shape, for bearing, argument and valour,
Goes foremost in report through Italy.

HERO

Indeed, he hath an excellent good name.

URSULA

His excellence did earn it, ere he had it.
When are you married, madam?

HERO

Why, every day, to-morrow. Come, go in:
I'll show thee some attires, and have thy counsel
Which is the best to furnish me to-morrow.

URSULA

She's limed, I warrant you: we have caught her, madam.

HERO

If it proves so, then loving goes by haps:
Some Cupid kills with arrows, some with traps.

Exeunt HERO and URSULA

BEATRICE

[Coming forward]
What fire is in mine ears? Can this be true?
Stand I condemn'd for pride and scorn so much?
Contempt, farewell! and maiden pride, adieu!
No glory lives behind the back of such.
And, Benedick, love on; I will requite thee,
Taming my wild heart to thy loving hand:
If thou dost love, my kindness shall incite thee
To bind our loves up in a holy band;
For others say thou dost deserve, and I
Believe it better than reportingly.

Exit

SCENE II.

A room in LEONATO'S house

Enter DON PEDRO, CLAUDIO, BENEDICK, and LEONATO

DON PEDRO

I do but stay till your marriage be consummate, and
then go I toward Arragon.

CLAUDIO

I'll bring you thither, my lord, if you'll
vouchsafe me.

DON PEDRO

Nay, that would be as great a soil in the new gloss
of your marriage as to show a child his new coat
and forbid him to wear it. I will only be bold
with Benedick for his company; for, from the crown
of his head to the sole of his foot, he is all
mirth: he hath twice or thrice cut Cupid's
bow-string and the little hangman dare not shoot at
him; he hath a heart as sound as a bell and his
tongue is the clapper, for what his heart thinks his
tongue speaks.

BENEDICK

Gallants, I am not as I have been.

LEONATO

So say I.. methinks you are sadder.

CLAUDIO

I hope he be in love.

DON PEDRO

Hang him, truant! there's no true drop of blood in
him, to be truly touched with love: if he be sad,
he wants money.

BENEDICK

I have the toothache.

DON PEDRO

Draw it.

BENEDICK

Hang it!

CLAUDIO

You must hang it first, and draw it afterwards.

DON PEDRO

What! sigh for the toothache?

LEONATO

Where is but a humour or a worm.

BENEDICK

Well, every one can master a grief but he that has
it.

CLAUDIO

Yet say I, he is in love.

DON PEDRO

There is no appearance of fancy in him, unless it be
a fancy that he hath to strange disguises; as, to be
a Dutchman today, a Frenchman to-morrow, or in the
shape of two countries at once, as, a German from
the waist downward, all slops, and a Spaniard from
the hip upward, no doublet. Unless he have a fancy
to this foolery, as it appears he hath, he is no
fool for fancy, as you would have it appear he is.

CLAUDIO

If he be not in love with some woman, there is no
believing old signs: a' brushes his hat o'
mornings; what should that bode?

DON PEDRO

Hath any man seen him at the barber's?

CLAUDIO

No, but the barber's man hath been seen with him,
and the old ornament of his cheek hath already
stuffed tennis-balls.

LEONATO

Indeed, he looks younger than he did, by the loss of a
beard.

DON PEDRO

Nay, a' rubs himself with civet: can you smell him
out by that?

CLAUDIO

That's as much as to say, the sweet youth's in love.

DON PEDRO

The greatest note of it is his melancholy.

CLAUDIO

And when was he wont to wash his face?

DON PEDRO

Yea, or to paint himself? for the which, I hear
what they say of him.

CLAUDIO

Nay, but his jesting spirit; which is now crept into
a lute-string and now governed by stops.

DON PEDRO

Indeed, that tells a heavy tale for him: conclude,
conclude he is in love.

CLAUDIO

Nay, but I know who loves him.

DON PEDRO

That would I know too: I warrant, one that knows him
not.

CLAUDIO

Yes, and his ill conditions; and, in despite of
all, dies for him.

DON PEDRO

She shall be buried with her face upwards.

BENEDICK

Yet is this no charm for the toothache. Old
signior, walk aside with me: I have studied eight

or nine wise words to speak to you, which these
hobby-horses must not hear.

Exeunt BENEDICK and LEONATO

DON PEDRO
For my life, to break with him about Beatrice.
CLAUDIO
'Tis even so. Hero and Margaret have by this
played their parts with Beatrice; and then the two
bears will not bite one another when they meet.

Enter DON JOHN

DON JOHN
My lord and brother, God save you!
DON PEDRO
Good den, brother.
DON JOHN
If your leisure served, I would speak with you.
DON PEDRO
In private?
DON JOHN
If it please you: yet Count Claudio may hear; for
what I would speak of concerns him.
DON PEDRO
What's the matter?
DON JOHN
[To CLAUDIO] Means your lordship to be married
to-morrow?
DON PEDRO
You know he does.
DON JOHN
I know not that, when he knows what I know.
CLAUDIO

If there be any impediment, I pray you discover it.

DON JOHN

You may think I love you not: let that appear
hereafter, and aim better at me by that I now will
manifest. For my brother, I think he holds you
well, and in dearness of heart hath holp to effect
your ensuing marriage;--surely suit ill spent and
labour ill bestowed.

DON PEDRO

Why, what's the matter?

DON JOHN

I came hither to tell you; and, circumstances
shortened, for she has been too long a talking of,
the lady is disloyal.

CLAUDIO

Who, Hero?

DON PEDRO

Even she; Leonato's Hero, your Hero, every man's Hero:

CLAUDIO

Disloyal?

DON JOHN

The word is too good to paint out her wickedness; I
could say she were worse: think you of a worse
title, and I will fit her to it. Wonder not till
further warrant: go but with me to-night, you shall
see her chamber-window entered, even the night
before her wedding-day: if you love her then,
to-morrow wed her; but it would better fit your honour
to change your mind.

CLAUDIO

May this be so?

DON PEDRO

I will not think it.

DON JOHN

If you dare not trust that you see, confess not
that you know: if you will follow me, I will show
you enough; and when you have seen more and heard
more, proceed accordingly.

CLAUDIO

If I see any thing to-night why I should not marry
her to-morrow in the congregation, where I should
wed, there will I shame her.

DON PEDRO

And, as I wooed for thee to obtain her, I will join
with thee to disgrace her.

DON JOHN

I will disparage her no farther till you are my
witnesses: bear it coldly but till midnight, and
let the issue show itself.

DON PEDRO

O day untowardly turned!

CLAUDIO

O mischief strangely thwarting!

DON JOHN

O plague right well prevented! so will you say when
you have seen the sequel.

Exeunt

SCENE III.

A street.

Enter DOGBERRY and VERGES with the Watch

DOGBERRY

Are you good men and true?

VERGES

Yea, or else it were pity but they should suffer
salvation, body and soul.

DOGBERRY

Nay, that were a punishment too good for them, if
they should have any allegiance in them, being
chosen for the prince's watch.

VERGES

Well, give them their charge, neighbour Dogberry.

DOGBERRY

First, who think you the most desertless man to be
constable?

First Watchman

Hugh Otecake, sir, or George Seacole; for they can
write and read.

DOGBERRY

Come hither, neighbour Seacole. God hath blessed
you with a good name: to be a well-favoured man is
the gift of fortune; but to write and read comes by
nature.

Second Watchman

Both which, master constable,--

DOGBERRY

You have: I knew it would be your answer. Well,
for your favour, sir, why, give God thanks, and make
no boast of it; and for your writing and reading,
let that appear when there is no need of such
vanity. You are thought here to be the most
senseless and fit man for the constable of the
watch; therefore bear you the lantern. This is your
charge: you shall comprehend all vagrom men; you are
to bid any man stand, in the prince's name.

Second Watchman

How if a' will not stand?

DOGBERRY

Why, then, take no note of him, but let him go; and
presently call the rest of the watch together and

thank God you are rid of a knave.

VERGES

If he will not stand when he is bidden, he is none
of the prince's subjects.

DOGBERRY

True, and they are to meddle with none but the
prince's subjects. You shall also make no noise in
the streets; for, for the watch to babble and to
talk is most tolerable and not to be endured.

Watchman

We will rather sleep than talk: we know what
belongs to a watch.

DOGBERRY

Why, you speak like an ancient and most quiet
watchman; for I cannot see how sleeping should
offend: only, have a care that your bills be not
stolen. Well, you are to call at all the
ale-houses, and bid those that are drunk get them to bed.

Watchman

How if they will not?

DOGBERRY

Why, then, let them alone till they are sober: if
they make you not then the better answer, you may
say they are not the men you took them for.

Watchman

Well, sir.

DOGBERRY

If you meet a thief, you may suspect him, by virtue
of your office, to be no true man; and, for such
kind of men, the less you meddle or make with them,
why the more is for your honesty.

Watchman

If we know him to be a thief, shall we not lay
hands on him?

DOGBERRY

Truly, by your office, you may; but I think they
that touch pitch will be defiled: the most peaceable
way for you, if you do take a thief, is to let him
show himself what he is and steal out of your company.

VERGES

You have been always called a merciful man, partner.

DOGBERRY

Truly, I would not hang a dog by my will, much more
a man who hath any honesty in him.

VERGES

If you hear a child cry in the night, you must call
to the nurse and bid her still it.

Watchman

How if the nurse be asleep and will not hear us?

DOGBERRY

Why, then, depart in peace, and let the child wake
her with crying; for the ewe that will not hear her
lamb when it baes will never answer a calf when he
bleats.

VERGES

'Tis very true.

DOGBERRY

This is the end of the charge:--you, constable, are
to present the prince's own person: if you meet the
prince in the night, you may stay him.

VERGES

Nay, by'r our lady, that I think a' cannot.

DOGBERRY

Five shillings to one on't, with any man that knows
the statutes, he may stay him: marry, not without
the prince be willing; for, indeed, the watch ought
to offend no man; and it is an offence to stay a
man against his will.

VERGES

By'r lady, I think it be so.

DOGBERRY

Ha, ha, ha! Well, masters, good night: an there be
any matter of weight chances, call up me: keep your
fellows' counsels and your own; and good night.
Come, neighbour.

Watchman

Well, masters, we hear our charge: let us go sit here
upon the church-bench till two, and then all to bed.

DOGBERRY

One word more, honest neighbours. I pray you watch
about Signior Leonato's door; for the wedding being
there to-morrow, there is a great coil to-night.
Adieu: be vigitant, I beseech you.

Exeunt DOGBERRY and VERGES

Enter BORACHIO and CONRADE

BORACHIO

What Conrade!

Watchman

[Aside] Peace! stir not.

BORACHIO

Conrade, I say!

CONRADE

Here, man; I am at thy elbow.

BORACHIO

Mass, and my elbow itched; I thought there would a
scab follow.

CONRADE

I will owe thee an answer for that: and now forward
with thy tale.

BORACHIO

Stand thee close, then, under this pent-house, for
it drizzles rain; and I will, like a true drunkard,
utter all to thee.

Watchman

[Aside] Some treason, masters: yet stand close.

BORACHIO

Therefore know I have earned of Don John a thousand
ducats.

CONRADE

Is it possible that any villany should be so dear?

BORACHIO

Thou shouldst rather ask if it were possible any
villany should be so rich; for when rich villains
have need of poor ones, poor ones may make what
price they will.

CONRADE

I wonder at it.

BORACHIO

That shows thou art unconfirmed. Thou knowest that
the fashion of a doublet, or a hat, or a cloak, is
nothing to a man.

CONRADE

Yes, it is apparel.

BORACHIO

I mean, the fashion.

CONRADE

Yes, the fashion is the fashion.

BORACHIO

Tush! I may as well say the fool's the fool. But
seest thou not what a deformed thief this fashion
is?

Watchman

[Aside] I know that Deformed; a' has been a vile

thief this seven year; a' goes up and down like a
gentleman: I remember his name.

BORACHIO

Didst thou not hear somebody?

CONRADE

No; 'twas the vane on the house.

BORACHIO

Seest thou not, I say, what a deformed thief this
fashion is? how giddily a' turns about all the hot
bloods between fourteen and five-and-thirty?
sometimes fashioning them like Pharaoh's soldiers
in the reeky painting, sometime like god Bel's
priests in the old church-window, sometime like the
shaven Hercules in the smirched worm-eaten tapestry,
where his codpiece seems as massy as his club?

CONRADE

All this I see; and I see that the fashion wears
out more apparel than the man. But art not thou
thyself giddy with the fashion too, that thou hast
shifted out of thy tale into telling me of the fashion?

BORACHIO

Not so, neither: but know that I have to-night
wooed Margaret, the Lady Hero's gentlewoman, by the
name of Hero: she leans me out at her mistress'
chamber-window, bids me a thousand times good
night,--I tell this tale vilely:--I should first
tell thee how the prince, Claudio and my master,
planted and placed and possessed by my master Don
John, saw afar off in the orchard this amiable encounter.

CONRADE

And thought they Margaret was Hero?

BORACHIO

Two of them did, the prince and Claudio; but the
devil my master knew she was Margaret; and partly

by his oaths, which first possessed them, partly by
the dark night, which did deceive them, but chiefly
by my villany, which did confirm any slander that
Don John had made, away went Claudio enraged; swore
he would meet her, as he was appointed, next morning
at the temple, and there, before the whole
congregation, shame her with what he saw o'er night
and send her home again without a husband.

First Watchman

We charge you, in the prince's name, stand!

Second Watchman

Call up the right master constable. We have here
recovered the most dangerous piece of lechery that
ever was known in the commonwealth.

First Watchman

And one Deformed is one of them: I know him; a'
wears a lock.

CONRADE

Masters, masters,--

Second Watchman

You'll be made bring Deformed forth, I warrant you.

CONRADE

Masters,--

First Watchman

Never speak: we charge you let us obey you to go with
us.

BORACHIO

We are like to prove a goodly commodity, being taken
up of these men's bills.

CONRADE

A commodity in question, I warrant you. Come, we'll
obey you.

Exeunt

SCENE IV.

HERO's apartment.

Enter HERO, MARGARET, and URSULA

HERO

Good Ursula, wake my cousin Beatrice, and desire
her to rise.

URSULA

I will, lady.

HERO

And bid her come hither.

URSULA

Well.

Exit

MARGARET

Troth, I think your other rabato were better.

HERO

No, pray thee, good Meg, I'll wear this.

MARGARET

By my troth, 's not so good; and I warrant your
cousin will say so.

HERO

My cousin's a fool, and thou art another: I'll wear
none but this.

MARGARET

I like the new tire within excellently, if the hair
were a thought browner; and your gown's a most rare
fashion, i' faith. I saw the Duchess of Milan's
gown that they praise so.

HERO

O, that exceeds, they say.

MARGARET

By my troth, 's but a night-gown in respect of

70

yours: cloth o' gold, and cuts, and laced with
silver, set with pearls, down sleeves, side sleeves,
and skirts, round underborne with a bluish tinsel:
but for a fine, quaint, graceful and excellent
fashion, yours is worth ten on 't.

HERO

God give me joy to wear it! for my heart is
exceeding heavy.

MARGARET

'Twill be heavier soon by the weight of a man.

HERO

Fie upon thee! art not ashamed?

MARGARET

Of what, lady? of speaking honourably? Is not
marriage honourable in a beggar? Is not your lord
honourable without marriage? I think you would have
me say, 'saving your reverence, a husband:' and bad
thinking do not wrest true speaking, I'll offend
nobody: is there any harm in 'the heavier for a
husband'? None, I think, and it be the right husband
and the right wife; otherwise 'tis light, and not
heavy: ask my Lady Beatrice else; here she comes.

Enter BEATRICE

HERO

Good morrow, coz.

BEATRICE

Good morrow, sweet Hero.

HERO

Why how now? do you speak in the sick tune?

BEATRICE

I am out of all other tune, methinks.

MARGARET

Clap's into 'Light o' love;' that goes without a

71

burden: do you sing it, and I'll dance it.

BEATRICE

Ye light o' love, with your heels! then, if your
husband have stables enough, you'll see he shall
lack no barns.

MARGARET

O illegitimate construction! I scorn that with my heels.

BEATRICE

'Tis almost five o'clock, cousin; tis time you were
ready. By my troth, I am exceeding ill: heigh-ho!

MARGARET

For a hawk, a horse, or a husband?

BEATRICE

For the letter that begins them all, H.

MARGARET

Well, and you be not turned Turk, there's no more
sailing by the star.

BEATRICE

What means the fool, trow?

MARGARET

Nothing I; but God send every one their heart's desire!

HERO

These gloves the count sent me; they are an
excellent perfume.

BEATRICE

I am stuffed, cousin; I cannot smell.

MARGARET

A maid, and stuffed! there's goodly catching of cold.

BEATRICE

O, God help me! God help me! how long have you
professed apprehension?

MARGARET

Even since you left it. Doth not my wit become me
rarely?

BEATRICE

It is not seen enough, you should wear it in your
cap. By my troth, I am sick.

MARGARET

Get you some of this distilled Carduus Benedictus,
and lay it to your heart: it is the only thing for a qualm.

HERO

There thou prickest her with a thistle.

BEATRICE

Benedictus! why Benedictus? you have some moral in
this Benedictus.

MARGARET

Moral! no, by my troth, I have no moral meaning; I
meant, plain holy-thistle. You may think perchance
that I think you are in love: nay, by'r lady, I am
not such a fool to think what I list, nor I list
not to think what I can, nor indeed I cannot think,
if I would think my heart out of thinking, that you
are in love or that you will be in love or that you
can be in love. Yet Benedick was such another, and
now is he become a man: he swore he would never
marry, and yet now, in despite of his heart, he eats
his meat without grudging: and how you may be
converted I know not, but methinks you look with
your eyes as other women do.

BEATRICE

What pace is this that thy tongue keeps?

MARGARET

Not a false gallop.

Re-enter URSULA

URSULA

Madam, withdraw: the prince, the count, Signior
Benedick, Don John, and all the gallants of the

town, are come to fetch you to church.

HERO

Help to dress me, good coz, good Meg, good Ursula.

Exeunt

SCENE V.

Another room in LEONATO'S house.

Enter LEONATO, with DOGBERRY and VERGES

LEONATO

What would you with me, honest neighbour?

DOGBERRY

Marry, sir, I would have some confidence with you
that decerns you nearly.

LEONATO

Brief, I pray you; for you see it is a busy time with me.

DOGBERRY

Marry, this it is, sir.

VERGES

Yes, in truth it is, sir.

LEONATO

What is it, my good friends?

DOGBERRY

Goodman Verges, sir, speaks a little off the
matter: an old man, sir, and his wits are not so
blunt as, God help, I would desire they were; but,
in faith, honest as the skin between his brows.

VERGES

Yes, I thank God I am as honest as any man living
that is an old man and no honester than I.

DOGBERRY

Comparisons are odorous: palabras, neighbour Verges.

LEONATO

Neighbours, you are tedious.

DOGBERRY

It pleases your worship to say so, but we are the
poor duke's officers; but truly, for mine own part,
if I were as tedious as a king, I could find it in
my heart to bestow it all of your worship.

LEONATO

All thy tediousness on me, ah?

DOGBERRY

Yea, an 'twere a thousand pound more than 'tis; for
I hear as good exclamation on your worship as of any
man in the city; and though I be but a poor man, I
am glad to hear it.

VERGES

And so am I.

LEONATO

I would fain know what you have to say.

VERGES

Marry, sir, our watch to-night, excepting your
worship's presence, ha' ta'en a couple of as arrant
knaves as any in Messina.

DOGBERRY

A good old man, sir; he will be talking: as they
say, when the age is in, the wit is out: God help
us! it is a world to see. Well said, i' faith,
neighbour Verges: well, God's a good man; an two men
ride of a horse, one must ride behind. An honest
soul, i' faith, sir; by my troth he is, as ever
broke bread; but God is to be worshipped; all men
are not alike; alas, good neighbour!

LEONATO

Indeed, neighbour, he comes too short of you.

DOGBERRY

Gifts that God gives.

LEONATO
  I must leave you.
DOGBERRY
  One word, sir: our watch, sir, have indeed
  comprehended two aspicious persons, and we would
  have them this morning examined before your worship.
LEONATO
  Take their examination yourself and bring it me: I
  am now in great haste, as it may appear unto you.
DOGBERRY
  It shall be suffigance.
LEONATO
  Drink some wine ere you go: fare you well.

Enter a Messenger

Messenger
  My lord, they stay for you to give your daughter to
  her husband.
LEONATO
  I'll wait upon them: I am ready.

Exeunt LEONATO and Messenger

DOGBERRY
  Go, good partner, go, get you to Francis Seacole;
  bid him bring his pen and inkhorn to the gaol: we
  are now to examination these men.
VERGES
  And we must do it wisely.
DOGBERRY
  We will spare for no wit, I warrant you; here's
  that shall drive some of them to a non-come: only
  get the learned writer to set down our
  excommunication and meet me at the gaol.

Exeunt

ACT IV

SCENE I.

A church.

Enter DON PEDRO, DON JOHN, LEONATO, FRIAR FRANCIS, CLAUDIO, BENEDICK, HERO, BEATRICE, and Attendants

LEONATO

Come, Friar Francis, be brief; only to the plain
form of marriage, and you shall recount their
particular duties afterwards.

FRIAR FRANCIS

You come hither, my lord, to marry this lady.

CLAUDIO

No.

LEONATO

To be married to her: friar, you come to marry her.

FRIAR FRANCIS

Lady, you come hither to be married to this count.

HERO

I do.

FRIAR FRANCIS

If either of you know any inward impediment why you
should not be conjoined, charge you, on your souls,
to utter it.

CLAUDIO

Know you any, Hero?

HERO

None, my lord.

FRIAR FRANCIS

Know you any, count?

LEONATO

I dare make his answer, none.

CLAUDIO

O, what men dare do! what men may do! what men daily

do, not knowing what they do!

BENEDICK

How now! interjections? Why, then, some be of laughing, as, ah, ha, he!

CLAUDIO

Stand thee by, friar. Father, by your leave:
Will you with free and unconstrained soul
Give me this maid, your daughter?

LEONATO

As freely, son, as God did give her me.

CLAUDIO

And what have I to give you back, whose worth
May counterpoise this rich and precious gift?

DON PEDRO

Nothing, unless you render her again.

CLAUDIO

Sweet prince, you learn me noble thankfulness.
There, Leonato, take her back again:
Give not this rotten orange to your friend;
She's but the sign and semblance of her honour.
Behold how like a maid she blushes here!
O, what authority and show of truth
Can cunning sin cover itself withal!
Comes not that blood as modest evidence
To witness simple virtue? Would you not swear,
All you that see her, that she were a maid,
By these exterior shows? But she is none:
She knows the heat of a luxurious bed;
Her blush is guiltiness, not modesty.

LEONATO

What do you mean, my lord?

CLAUDIO

Not to be married,
Not to knit my soul to an approved wanton.

LEONATO

Dear my lord, if you, in your own proof,
Have vanquish'd the resistance of her youth,
And made defeat of her virginity,--

CLAUDIO

I know what you would say: if I have known her,
You will say she did embrace me as a husband,
And so extenuate the 'forehand sin:
No, Leonato,
I never tempted her with word too large;
But, as a brother to his sister, show'd
Bashful sincerity and comely love.

HERO

And seem'd I ever otherwise to you?

CLAUDIO

Out on thee! Seeming! I will write against it:
You seem to me as Dian in her orb,
As chaste as is the bud ere it be blown;
But you are more intemperate in your blood
Than Venus, or those pamper'd animals
That rage in savage sensuality.

HERO

Is my lord well, that he doth speak so wide?

LEONATO

Sweet prince, why speak not you?

DON PEDRO

What should I speak?
I stand dishonour'd, that have gone about
To link my dear friend to a common stale.

LEONATO

Are these things spoken, or do I but dream?

DON JOHN

Sir, they are spoken, and these things are true.

BENEDICK

This looks not like a nuptial.

HERO

True! O God!

CLAUDIO

Leonato, stand I here?

Is this the prince? is this the prince's brother?

Is this face Hero's? are our eyes our own?

LEONATO

All this is so: but what of this, my lord?

CLAUDIO

Let me but move one question to your daughter;

And, by that fatherly and kindly power

That you have in her, bid her answer truly.

LEONATO

I charge thee do so, as thou art my child.

HERO

O, God defend me! how am I beset!

What kind of catechising call you this?

CLAUDIO

To make you answer truly to your name.

HERO

Is it not Hero? Who can blot that name

With any just reproach?

CLAUDIO

Marry, that can Hero;

Hero itself can blot out Hero's virtue.

What man was he talk'd with you yesternight

Out at your window betwixt twelve and one?

Now, if you are a maid, answer to this.

HERO

I talk'd with no man at that hour, my lord.

DON PEDRO

Why, then are you no maiden. Leonato,
I am sorry you must hear: upon mine honour,
Myself, my brother and this grieved count
Did see her, hear her, at that hour last night
Talk with a ruffian at her chamber-window
Who hath indeed, most like a liberal villain,
Confess'd the vile encounters they have had
A thousand times in secret.

DON JOHN

Fie, fie! they are not to be named, my lord,
Not to be spoke of;
There is not chastity enough in language
Without offence to utter them. Thus, pretty lady,
I am sorry for thy much misgovernment.

CLAUDIO

O Hero, what a Hero hadst thou been,
If half thy outward graces had been placed
About thy thoughts and counsels of thy heart!
But fare thee well, most foul, most fair! farewell,
Thou pure impiety and impious purity!
For thee I'll lock up all the gates of love,
And on my eyelids shall conjecture hang,
To turn all beauty into thoughts of harm,
And never shall it more be gracious.

LEONATO

Hath no man's dagger here a point for me?

HERO swoons

BEATRICE

Why, how now, cousin! wherefore sink you down?

DON JOHN

Come, let us go. These things, come thus to light,

Smother her spirits up.

Exeunt DON PEDRO, DON JOHN, and CLAUDIO

BENEDICK
  How doth the lady?
BEATRICE
  Dead, I think. Help, uncle!
  Hero! why, Hero! Uncle! Signior Benedick! Friar!
LEONATO
  O Fate! take not away thy heavy hand.
  Death is the fairest cover for her shame
  That may be wish'd for.
BEATRICE
  How now, cousin Hero!
FRIAR FRANCIS
  Have comfort, lady.
LEONATO
  Dost thou look up?
FRIAR FRANCIS
  Yea, wherefore should she not?
LEONATO
  Wherefore! Why, doth not every earthly thing
  Cry shame upon her? Could she here deny
  The story that is printed in her blood?
  Do not live, Hero; do not ope thine eyes:
  For, did I think thou wouldst not quickly die,
  Thought I thy spirits were stronger than thy shames,
  Myself would, on the rearward of reproaches,
  Strike at thy life. Grieved I, I had but one?
  Chid I for that at frugal nature's frame?
  O, one too much by thee! Why had I one?
  Why ever wast thou lovely in my eyes?
  Why had I not with charitable hand
  Took up a beggar's issue at my gates,

Who smirch'd thus and mired with infamy,
I might have said 'No part of it is mine;
This shame derives itself from unknown loins'?
But mine and mine I loved and mine I praised
And mine that I was proud on, mine so much
That I myself was to myself not mine,
Valuing of her,--why, she, O, she is fallen
Into a pit of ink, that the wide sea
Hath drops too few to wash her clean again
And salt too little which may season give
To her foul-tainted flesh!

BENEDICK

Sir, sir, be patient.
For my part, I am so attired in wonder,
I know not what to say.

BEATRICE

O, on my soul, my cousin is belied!

BENEDICK

Lady, were you her bedfellow last night?

BEATRICE

No, truly not; although, until last night,
I have this twelvemonth been her bedfellow.

LEONATO

Confirm'd, confirm'd! O, that is stronger made
Which was before barr'd up with ribs of iron!
Would the two princes lie, and Claudio lie,
Who loved her so, that, speaking of her foulness,
Wash'd it with tears? Hence from her! let her die.

FRIAR FRANCIS

Hear me a little;
For I have only been silent so long
And given way unto this course of fortune.
...
By noting of the lady I have mark'd

A thousand blushing apparitions
To start into her face, a thousand innocent shames
In angel whiteness beat away those blushes;
And in her eye there hath appear'd a fire,
To burn the errors that these princes hold
Against her maiden truth. Call me a fool;
Trust not my reading nor my observations,
Which with experimental seal doth warrant
The tenor of my book; trust not my age,
My reverence, calling, nor divinity,
If this sweet lady lie not guiltless here
Under some biting error.

LEONATO

Friar, it cannot be.
Thou seest that all the grace that she hath left
Is that she will not add to her damnation
A sin of perjury; she not denies it:
Why seek'st thou then to cover with excuse
That which appears in proper nakedness?

FRIAR FRANCIS

Lady, what man is he you are accused of?

HERO

They know that do accuse me; I know none:
If I know more of any man alive
Than that which maiden modesty doth warrant,
Let all my sins lack mercy! O my father,
Prove you that any man with me conversed
At hours unmeet, or that I yesternight
Maintain'd the change of words with any creature,
Refuse me, hate me, torture me to death!

FRIAR FRANCIS

There is some strange misprision in the princes.

BENEDICK

Two of them have the very bent of honour;

And if their wisdoms be misled in this,
The practise of it lives in John the bastard,
Whose spirits toil in frame of villanies.
LEONATO
I know not. If they speak but truth of her,
These hands shall tear her; if they wrong her honour,
The proudest of them shall well hear of it.
Time hath not yet so dried this blood of mine,
Nor age so eat up my invention,
Nor fortune made such havoc of my means,
Nor my bad life reft me so much of friends,
But they shall find, awaked in such a kind,
Both strength of limb and policy of mind,
Ability in means and choice of friends,
To quit me of them throughly.
FRIAR FRANCIS
Pause awhile,
And let my counsel sway you in this case.
Your daughter here the princes left for dead:
Let her awhile be secretly kept in,
And publish it that she is dead indeed;
Maintain a mourning ostentation
And on your family's old monument
Hang mournful epitaphs and do all rites
That appertain unto a burial.
LEONATO
What shall become of this? what will this do?
FRIAR FRANCIS
Marry, this well carried shall on her behalf
Change slander to remorse; that is some good:
But not for that dream I on this strange course,
But on this travail look for greater birth.
She dying, as it must so be maintain'd,
Upon the instant that she was accused,

Shall be lamented, pitied and excused
Of every hearer: for it so falls out
That what we have we prize not to the worth
Whiles we enjoy it, but being lack'd and lost,
Why, then we rack the value, then we find
The virtue that possession would not show us
Whiles it was ours. So will it fare with Claudio:
When he shall hear she died upon his words,
The idea of her life shall sweetly creep
Into his study of imagination,
And every lovely organ of her life
Shall come apparell'd in more precious habit,
More moving-delicate and full of life,
Into the eye and prospect of his soul,
Than when she lived indeed; then shall he mourn,
If ever love had interest in his liver,
And wish he had not so accused her,
No, though he thought his accusation true.
Lct this be so, and doubt not but success
Will fashion the event in better shape
Than I can lay it down in likelihood.
But if all aim but this be levell'd false,
The supposition of the lady's death
Will quench the wonder of her infamy:
And if it sort not well, you may conceal her,
As best befits her wounded reputation,
In some reclusive and religious life,
Out of all eyes, tongues, minds and injuries.
BENEDICK
Signior Leonato, let the friar advise you:
And though you know my inwardness and love
Is very much unto the prince and Claudio,
Yet, by mine honour, I will deal in this
As secretly and justly as your soul

Should with your body.

LEONATO

Being that I flow in grief,

The smallest twine may lead me.

FRIAR FRANCIS

'Tis well consented: presently away;

For to strange sores strangely they strain the cure.

Come, lady, die to live: this wedding-day

Perhaps is but prolong'd: have patience and endure.

Exeunt all but BENEDICK and BEATRICE

BENEDICK

Lady Beatrice, have you wept all this while?

BEATRICE

Yea, and I will weep a while longer.

BENEDICK

I will not desire that.

BEATRICE

You have no reason; I do it freely.

BENEDICK

Surely I do believe your fair cousin is wronged.

BEATRICE

Ah, how much might the man deserve of me that would right her!

BENEDICK

Is there any way to show such friendship?

BEATRICE

A very even way, but no such friend.

BENEDICK

May a man do it?

BEATRICE

It is a man's office, but not yours.

BENEDICK

I do love nothing in the world so well as you: is

not that strange?

BEATRICE

As strange as the thing I know not. It were as
possible for me to say I loved nothing so well as
you: but believe me not; and yet I lie not; I
confess nothing, nor I deny nothing. I am sorry for my
cousin.

BENEDICK

By my sword, Beatrice, thou lovest me.

BEATRICE

Do not swear, and eat it.

BENEDICK

I will swear by it that you love me; and I will make
him eat it that says I love not you.

BEATRICE

Will you not eat your word?

BENEDICK

With no sauce that can be devised to it. I protest
I love thee.

BEATRICE

Why, then, God forgive me!

BENEDICK

What offence, sweet Beatrice?

BEATRICE

You have stayed me in a happy hour: I was about to
protest I loved you.

BENEDICK

And do it with all thy heart.

BEATRICE

I love you with so much of my heart that none is
left to protest.

BENEDICK

Come, bid me do any thing for thee.

BEATRICE

Kill Claudio.
BENEDICK

Ha! not for the wide world.
BEATRICE

You kill me to deny it. Farewell.
BENEDICK

Tarry, sweet Beatrice.
BEATRICE

I am gone, though I am here: there is no love in
you: nay, I pray you, let me go.
BENEDICK

Beatrice,--
BEATRICE

In faith, I will go.
BENEDICK

We'll be friends first.
BEATRICE

You dare easier be friends with me than fight with mine
enemy.
BENEDICK

Is Claudio thine enemy?
BEATRICE

Is he not approved in the height a villain, that
hath slandered, scorned, dishonoured my kinswoman? O
that I were a man! What, bear her in hand until they
come to take hands; and then, with public
accusation, uncovered slander, unmitigated rancour,
--O God, that I were a man! I would eat his heart
in the market-place.
BENEDICK

Hear me, Beatrice,--
BEATRICE

Talk with a man out at a window! A proper saying!
BENEDICK

Nay, but, Beatrice,--
BEATRICE
Sweet Hero! She is wronged, she is slandered, she is
undone.
BENEDICK
Beat--
BEATRICE
Princes and counties! Surely, a princely testimony,
a goodly count, Count Comfect; a sweet gallant,
surely! O that I were a man for his sake! or that I
had any friend would be a man for my sake! But
manhood is melted into courtesies, valour into
compliment, and men are only turned into tongue, and
trim ones too: he is now as valiant as Hercules
that only tells a lie and swears it. I cannot be a
man with wishing, therefore I will die a woman with
grieving.
BENEDICK
Tarry, good Beatrice. By this hand, I love thee.
BEATRICE
Use it for my love some other way than swearing by it.
BENEDICK
Think you in your soul the Count Claudio hath wronged
Hero?
BEATRICE
Yea, as sure as I have a thought or a soul.
BENEDICK
Enough, I am engaged; I will challenge him. I will
kiss your hand, and so I leave you. By this hand,
Claudio shall render me a dear account. As you
hear of me, so think of me. Go, comfort your
cousin: I must say she is dead: and so, farewell.

Exeunt

SCENE II.

A prison.

Enter DOGBERRY, VERGES, and Sexton, in gowns; and the Watch, with CONRADE and BORACHIO

DOGBERRY

Is our whole dissembly appeared?

VERGES

O, a stool and a cushion for the sexton.

Sexton

Which be the malefactors?

DOGBERRY

Marry, that am I and my partner.

VERGES

Nay, that's certain; we have the exhibition to examine.

Sexton

But which are the offenders that are to be
examined? let them come before master constable.

DOGBERRY

Yea, marry, let them come before me. What is your
name, friend?

BORACHIO

Borachio.

DOGBERRY

Pray, write down, Borachio. Yours, sirrah?

CONRADE

I am a gentleman, sir, and my name is Conrade.

DOGBERRY

Write down, master gentleman Conrade. Masters, do
you serve God?

CONRADE BORACHIO

Yea, sir, we hope.

DOGBERRY

Write down, that they hope they serve God: and

write God first; for God defend but God should go
before such villains! Masters, it is proved already
that you are little better than false knaves; and it
will go near to be thought so shortly. How answer
you for yourselves?

CONRADE

Marry, sir, we say we are none.

DOGBERRY

A marvellous witty fellow, I assure you: but I
will go about with him. Come you hither, sirrah; a
word in your ear: sir, I say to you, it is thought
you are false knaves.

BORACHIO

Sir, I say to you we are none.

DOGBERRY

Well, stand aside. 'Fore God, they are both in a
tale. Have you writ down, that they are none?

Sexton

Master constable, you go not the way to examine:
you must call forth the watch that are their accusers.

DOGBERRY

Yea, marry, that's the eftest way. Let the watch
come forth. Masters, I charge you, in the prince's
name, accuse these men.

First Watchman

This man said, sir, that Don John, the prince's
brother, was a villain.

DOGBERRY

Write down Prince John a villain. Why, this is flat
perjury, to call a prince's brother villain.

BORACHIO

Master constable,--

DOGBERRY

Pray thee, fellow, peace: I do not like thy look,

I promise thee.

Sexton

What heard you him say else?

Second Watchman

Marry, that he had received a thousand ducats of
Don John for accusing the Lady Hero wrongfully.

DOGBERRY

Flat burglary as ever was committed.

VERGES

Yea, by mass, that it is.

Sexton

What else, fellow?

First Watchman

And that Count Claudio did mean, upon his words, to
disgrace Hero before the whole assembly. and not marry
her.

DOGBERRY

O villain! thou wilt be condemned into everlasting
redemption for this.

Sexton

What else?

Watchman

This is all.

Sexton

And this is more, masters, than you can deny.
Prince John is this morning secretly stolen away;
Hero was in this manner accused, in this very manner
refused, and upon the grief of this suddenly died.
Master constable, let these men be bound, and
brought to Leonato's: I will go before and show
him their examination.

Exit

DOGBERRY

Come, let them be opinioned.

VERGES

Let them be in the hands--

CONRADE

Off, coxcomb!

DOGBERRY

God's my life, where's the sexton? let him write
down the prince's officer coxcomb. Come, bind them.
Thou naughty varlet!

CONRADE

Away! you are an ass, you are an ass.

DOGBERRY

Dost thou not suspect my place? dost thou not
suspect my years? O that he were here to write me
down an ass! But, masters, remember that I am an
ass; though it be not written down, yet forget not
that I am an ass. No, thou villain, thou art full of
piety, as shall be proved upon thee by good witness.
I am a wise fellow, and, which is more, an officer,
and, which is more, a householder, and, which is
more, as pretty a piece of flesh as any is in
Messina, and one that knows the law, go to; and a
rich fellow enough, go to; and a fellow that hath
had losses, and one that hath two gowns and every
thing handsome about him. Bring him away. O that
I had been writ down an ass!

Exeunt

ACT V

SCENE I.

Before LEONATO'S house.

Enter LEONATO and ANTONIO

ANTONIO

If you go on thus, you will kill yourself:
And 'tis not wisdom thus to second grief
Against yourself.

LEONATO

I pray thee, cease thy counsel,
Which falls into mine ears as profitless
As water in a sieve: give not me counsel;
Nor let no comforter delight mine ear
But such a one whose wrongs do suit with mine.
Bring me a father that so loved his child,
Whose joy of her is overwhelm'd like mine,
And bid him speak of patience;
Measure his woe the length and breadth of mine
And let it answer every strain for strain,
As thus for thus and such a grief for such,
In every lineament, branch, shape, and form:
If such a one will smile and stroke his beard,
Bid sorrow wag, cry 'hem!' when he should groan,
Patch grief with proverbs, make misfortune drunk
With candle-wasters; bring him yet to me,
And I of him will gather patience.
But there is no such man: for, brother, men
Can counsel and speak comfort to that grief
Which they themselves not feel; but, tasting it,
Their counsel turns to passion, which before
Would give preceptial medicine to rage,

Fetter strong madness in a silken thread,
Charm ache with air and agony with words:
No, no; 'tis all men's office to speak patience
To those that wring under the load of sorrow,
But no man's virtue nor sufficiency
To be so moral when he shall endure
The like himself. Therefore give me no counsel:
My griefs cry louder than advertisement.
ANTONIO
Therein do men from children nothing differ.
LEONATO
I pray thee, peace. I will be flesh and blood;
For there was never yet philosopher
That could endure the toothache patiently,
However they have writ the style of gods
And made a push at chance and sufferance.
ANTONIO
Yet bend not all the harm upon yourself;
Make those that do offend you suffer too.
LEONATO
There thou speak'st reason: nay, I will do so.
My soul doth tell me Hero is belied;
And that shall Claudio know; so shall the prince
And all of them that thus dishonour her.
ANTONIO
Here comes the prince and Claudio hastily.

Enter DON PEDRO and CLAUDIO

DON PEDRO
Good den, good den.
CLAUDIO
Good day to both of you.
LEONATO
Hear you. my lords,--

DON PEDRO
  We have some haste, Leonato.
LEONATO
  Some haste, my lord! well, fare you well, my lord:
  Are you so hasty now? well, all is one.
DON PEDRO
  Nay, do not quarrel with us, good old man.
ANTONIO
  If he could right himself with quarreling,
  Some of us would lie low.
CLAUDIO
  Who wrongs him?
LEONATO
  Marry, thou dost wrong me; thou dissembler, thou:--
  Nay, never lay thy hand upon thy sword;
  I fear thee not.
CLAUDIO
  Marry, beshrew my hand,
  If it should give your age such cause of fear:
  In faith, my hand meant nothing to my sword.
LEONATO
  Tush, tush, man; never fleer and jest at me:
  I speak not like a dotard nor a fool,
  As under privilege of age to brag
  What I have done being young, or what would do
  Were I not old. Know, Claudio, to thy head,
  Thou hast so wrong'd mine innocent child and me
  That I am forced to lay my reverence by
  And, with grey hairs and bruise of many days,
  Do challenge thee to trial of a man.
  I say thou hast belied mine innocent child;
  Thy slander hath gone through and through her heart,
  And she lies buried with her ancestors;
  O, in a tomb where never scandal slept,

Save this of hers, framed by thy villany!
CLAUDIO
  My villany?
LEONATO
  Thine, Claudio; thine, I say.
DON PEDRO
  You say not right, old man.
LEONATO
  My lord, my lord,
  I'll prove it on his body, if he dare,
  Despite his nice fence and his active practise,
  His May of youth and bloom of lustihood.
CLAUDIO
  Away! I will not have to do with you.
LEONATO
  Canst thou so daff me? Thou hast kill'd my child:
  If thou kill'st me, boy, thou shalt kill a man.
ANTONIO
  He shall kill two of us, and men indeed:
  But that's no matter; let him kill one first;
  Win me and wear me; let him answer me.
  Come, follow me, boy; come, sir boy, come, follow me:
  Sir boy, I'll whip you from your foining fence;
  Nay, as I am a gentleman, I will.
LEONATO
  Brother,--
ANTONIO
  Content yourself. God knows I loved my niece;
  And she is dead, slander'd to death by villains,
  That dare as well answer a man indeed
  As I dare take a serpent by the tongue:
  Boys, apes, braggarts, Jacks, milksops!
LEONATO
  Brother Antony,--

ANTONIO

Hold you content. What, man! I know them, yea,
And what they weigh, even to the utmost scruple,--
Scrambling, out-facing, fashion-monging boys,
That lie and cog and flout, deprave and slander,
Go anticly, show outward hideousness,
And speak off half a dozen dangerous words,
How they might hurt their enemies, if they durst;
And this is all.

LEONATO

But, brother Antony,--

ANTONIO

Come, 'tis no matter:
Do not you meddle; let me deal in this.

DON PEDRO

Gentlemen both, we will not wake your patience.
My heart is sorry for your daughter's death:
But, on my honour, she was charged with nothing
But what was true and very full of proof.

LEONATO

My lord, my lord,--

DON PEDRO

I will not hear you.

LEONATO

No? Come, brother; away! I will be heard.

ANTONIO

And shall, or some of us will smart for it.

Exeunt LEONATO and ANTONIO

DON PEDRO

See, see; here comes the man we went to seek.

Enter BENEDICK

CLAUDIO

Now, signior, what news?

BENEDICK

Good day, my lord.

DON PEDRO

Welcome, signior: you are almost come to part
almost a fray.

CLAUDIO

We had like to have had our two noses snapped off
with two old men without teeth.

DON PEDRO

Leonato and his brother. What thinkest thou? Had
we fought, I doubt we should have been too young for
them.

BENEDICK

In a false quarrel there is no true valour. I came
to seek you both.

CLAUDIO

We have been up and down to seek thee; for we are
high-proof melancholy and would fain have it beaten
away. Wilt thou use thy wit?

BENEDICK

It is in my scabbard: shall I draw it?

DON PEDRO

Dost thou wear thy wit by thy side?

CLAUDIO

Never any did so, though very many have been beside
their wit. I will bid thee draw, as we do the
minstrels; draw, to pleasure us.

DON PEDRO

As I am an honest man, he looks pale. Art thou
sick, or angry?

CLAUDIO

What, courage, man! What though care killed a cat,

thou hast mettle enough in thee to kill care.

BENEDICK

Sir, I shall meet your wit in the career, and you
charge it against me. I pray you choose another subject.

CLAUDIO

Nay, then, give him another staff: this last was
broke cross.

DON PEDRO

By this light, he changes more and more: I think
he be angry indeed.

CLAUDIO

If he be, he knows how to turn his girdle.

BENEDICK

Shall I speak a word in your ear?

CLAUDIO

God bless me from a challenge!

BENEDICK

[Aside to CLAUDIO] You are a villain; I jest not:
I will make it good how you dare, with what you
dare, and when you dare. Do me right, or I will
protest your cowardice. You have killed a sweet
lady, and her death shall fall heavy on you. Let me
hear from you.

CLAUDIO

Well, I will meet you, so I may have good cheer.

DON PEDRO

What, a feast, a feast?

CLAUDIO

I' faith, I thank him; he hath bid me to a calf's
head and a capon; the which if I do not carve most
curiously, say my knife's naught. Shall I not find
a woodcock too?

BENEDICK

Sir, your wit ambles well; it goes easily.

DON PEDRO

I'll tell thee how Beatrice praised thy wit the
other day. I said, thou hadst a fine wit: 'True,'
said she, 'a fine little one.' 'No,' said I, 'a
great wit:' 'Right,' says she, 'a great gross one.'
'Nay,' said I, 'a good wit:' 'Just,' said she, 'it
hurts nobody.' 'Nay,' said I, 'the gentleman
is wise:' 'Certain,' said she, 'a wise gentleman.'
'Nay,' said I, 'he hath the tongues:' 'That I
believe,' said she, 'for he swore a thing to me on
Monday night, which he forswore on Tuesday morning;
there's a double tongue; there's two tongues.' Thus
did she, an hour together, transshape thy particular
virtues: yet at last she concluded with a sigh, thou
wast the properest man in Italy.

CLAUDIO

For the which she wept heartily and said she cared
not.

DON PEDRO

Yea, that she did: but yet, for all that, an if she
did not hate him deadly, she would love him dearly:
the old man's daughter told us all.

CLAUDIO

All, all; and, moreover, God saw him when he was
hid in the garden.

DON PEDRO

But when shall we set the savage bull's horns on
the sensible Benedick's head?

CLAUDIO

Yea, and text underneath, 'Here dwells Benedick the
married man'?

BENEDICK

Fare you well, boy: you know my mind. I will leave
you now to your gossip-like humour: you break jests

as braggarts do their blades, which God be thanked,
hurt not. My lord, for your many courtesies I thank
you: I must discontinue your company: your brother
the bastard is fled from Messina: you have among
you killed a sweet and innocent lady. For my Lord
Lackbeard there, he and I shall meet: and, till
then, peace be with him.

Exit

DON PEDRO
He is in earnest.
CLAUDIO
In most profound earnest; and, I'll warrant you, for
the love of Beatrice.
DON PEDRO
And hath challenged thee.
CLAUDIO
Most sincerely.
DON PEDRO
What a pretty thing man is when he goes in his
doublet and hose and leaves off his wit!
CLAUDIO
He is then a giant to an ape; but then is an ape a
doctor to such a man.
DON PEDRO
But, soft you, let me be: pluck up, my heart, and
be sad. Did he not say, my brother was fled?

*Enter DOGBERRY, VERGES, and the Watch, with
CONRADE and BORACHIO*

DOGBERRY
Come you, sir: if justice cannot tame you, she
shall ne'er weigh more reasons in her balance: nay,

an you be a cursing hypocrite once, you must be looked
to.

DON PEDRO

How now? two of my brother's men bound! Borachio
one!

CLAUDIO

Hearken after their offence, my lord.

DON PEDRO

Officers, what offence have these men done?

DOGBERRY

Marry, sir, they have committed false report;
moreover, they have spoken untruths; secondarily,
they are slanders; sixth and lastly, they have
belied a lady; thirdly, they have verified unjust
things; and, to conclude, they are lying knaves.

DON PEDRO

First, I ask thee what they have done; thirdly, I
ask thee what's their offence; sixth and lastly, why
they are committed; and, to conclude, what you lay
to their charge.

CLAUDIO

Rightly reasoned, and in his own division: and, by
my troth, there's one meaning well suited.

DON PEDRO

Who have you offended, masters, that you are thus
bound to your answer? this learned constable is
too cunning to be understood: what's your offence?

BORACHIO

Sweet prince, let me go no farther to mine answer:
do you hear me, and let this count kill me. I have
deceived even your very eyes: what your wisdoms
could not discover, these shallow fools have brought
to light: who in the night overheard me confessing
to this man how Don John your brother incensed me

104

to slander the Lady Hero, how you were brought into
the orchard and saw me court Margaret in Hero's
garments, how you disgraced her, when you should
marry her: my villany they have upon record; which
I had rather seal with my death than repeat over
to my shame. The lady is dead upon mine and my
master's false accusation; and, briefly, I desire
nothing but the reward of a villain.

DON PEDRO

Runs not this speech like iron through your blood?

CLAUDIO

I have drunk poison whiles he utter'd it.

DON PEDRO

But did my brother set thee on to this?

BORACHIO

Yea, and paid me richly for the practise of it.

DON PEDRO

He is composed and framed of treachery:
And fled he is upon this villany.

CLAUDIO

Sweet Hero! now thy image doth appear
In the rare semblance that I loved it first.

DOGBERRY

Come, bring away the plaintiffs: by this time our
sexton hath reformed Signior Leonato of the matter:
and, masters, do not forget to specify, when time
and place shall serve, that I am an ass.

VERGES

Here, here comes master Signior Leonato, and the
Sexton too.

Re-enter LEONATO and ANTONIO, with the Sexton

LEONATO

Which is the villain? let me see his eyes,

That, when I note another man like him,
I may avoid him: which of these is he?
BORACHIO
If you would know your wronger, look on me.
LEONATO
Art thou the slave that with thy breath hast kill'd
Mine innocent child?
BORACHIO
Yea, even I alone.
LEONATO
No, not so, villain; thou beliest thyself:
Here stand a pair of honourable men;
A third is fled, that had a hand in it.
I thank you, princes, for my daughter's death:
Record it with your high and worthy deeds:
'Twas bravely done, if you bethink you of it.
CLAUDIO
I know not how to pray your patience;
Yet I must speak. Choose your revenge yourself;
Impose me to what penance your invention
Can lay upon my sin: yet sinn'd I not
But in mistaking.
DON PEDRO
By my soul, nor I:
And yet, to satisfy this good old man,
I would bend under any heavy weight
That he'll enjoin me to.
LEONATO
I cannot bid you bid my daughter live;
That were impossible: but, I pray you both,
Possess the people in Messina here
How innocent she died; and if your love
Can labour ought in sad invention,
Hang her an epitaph upon her tomb

And sing it to her bones, sing it to-night:
To-morrow morning come you to my house,
And since you could not be my son-in-law,
Be yet my nephew: my brother hath a daughter,
Almost the copy of my child that's dead,
And she alone is heir to both of us:
Give her the right you should have given her cousin,
And so dies my revenge.

CLAUDIO

O noble sir,
Your over-kindness doth wring tears from me!
I do embrace your offer; and dispose
For henceforth of poor Claudio.

LEONATO

To-morrow then I will expect your coming;
To-night I take my leave. This naughty man
Shall face to face be brought to Margaret,
Who I believe was pack'd in all this wrong,
Hired to it by your brother.

BORACHIO

No, by my soul, she was not,
Nor knew not what she did when she spoke to me,
But always hath been just and virtuous
In any thing that I do know by her.

DOGBERRY

Moreover, sir, which indeed is not under white and
black, this plaintiff here, the offender, did call
me ass: I beseech you, let it be remembered in his
punishment. And also, the watch heard them talk of
one Deformed: they say be wears a key in his ear and
a lock hanging by it, and borrows money in God's
name, the which he hath used so long and never paid
that now men grow hard-hearted and will lend nothing
for God's sake: pray you, examine him upon that point.

LEONATO

I thank thee for thy care and honest pains.

DOGBERRY

Your worship speaks like a most thankful and
reverend youth; and I praise God for you.

LEONATO

There's for thy pains.

DOGBERRY

God save the foundation!

LEONATO

Go, I discharge thee of thy prisoner, and I thank thee.

DOGBERRY

I leave an arrant knave with your worship; which I
beseech your worship to correct yourself, for the
example of others. God keep your worship! I wish
your worship well; God restore you to health! I
humbly give you leave to depart; and if a merry
meeting may be wished, God prohibit it! Come,
neighbour.

Exeunt DOGBERRY and VERGES

LEONATO

Until to-morrow morning, lords, farewell.

ANTONIO

Farewell, my lords: we look for you to-morrow.

DON PEDRO

We will not fail.

CLAUDIO

To-night I'll mourn with Hero.

LEONATO

[To the Watch] Bring you these fellows on. We'll
talk with Margaret,
How her acquaintance grew with this lewd fellow.

Exeunt, severally

SCENE II.

LEONATO'S garden.

Enter BENEDICK and MARGARET, meeting

BENEDICK

Pray thee, sweet Mistress Margaret, deserve well at
my hands by helping me to the speech of Beatrice.

MARGARET

Will you then write me a sonnet in praise of my beauty?

BENEDICK

In so high a style, Margaret, that no man living
shall come over it; for, in most comely truth, thou
deservest it.

MARGARET

To have no man come over me! why, shall I always
keep below stairs?

BENEDICK

Thy wit is as quick as the greyhound's mouth; it catches.

MARGARET

And yours as blunt as the fencer's foils, which hit,
but hurt not.

BENEDICK

A most manly wit, Margaret; it will not hurt a
woman: and so, I pray thee, call Beatrice: I give
thee the bucklers.

MARGARET

Give us the swords; we have bucklers of our own.

BENEDICK

If you use them, Margaret, you must put in the
pikes with a vice; and they are dangerous weapons for
maids.

MARGARET

Well, I will call Beatrice to you, who I think hath legs.

BENEDICK

And therefore will come.

Exit MARGARET

Sings

The god of love,
That sits above,
And knows me, and knows me,
How pitiful I deserve,--
I mean in singing; but in loving, Leander the good
swimmer, Troilus the first employer of panders, and
a whole bookful of these quondam carpet-mangers,
whose names yet run smoothly in the even road of a
blank verse, why, they were never so truly turned
over and over as my poor self in love. Marry, I
cannot show it in rhyme; I have tried: I can find
out no rhyme to 'lady' but 'baby,' an innocent
rhyme; for 'scorn,' 'horn,' a hard rhyme; for,
'school,' 'fool,' a babbling rhyme; very ominous
endings: no, I was not born under a rhyming planet,
nor I cannot woo in festival terms.

Enter BEATRICE

Sweet Beatrice, wouldst thou come when I called thee?
BEATRICE
    Yea, signior, and depart when you bid me.
BENEDICK
    O, stay but till then!
BEATRICE
    'Then' is spoken; fare you well now: and yet, ere
    I go, let me go with that I came; which is, with
    knowing what hath passed between you and Claudio.
BENEDICK

Only foul words; and thereupon I will kiss thee.
BEATRICE

Foul words is but foul wind, and foul wind is but
foul breath, and foul breath is noisome; therefore I
will depart unkissed.
BENEDICK

Thou hast frighted the word out of his right sense,
so forcible is thy wit. But I must tell thee
plainly, Claudio undergoes my challenge; and either
I must shortly hear from him, or I will subscribe
him a coward. And, I pray thee now, tell me for
which of my bad parts didst thou first fall in love with
me?
BEATRICE

For them all together; which maintained so politic
a state of evil that they will not admit any good
part to intermingle with them. But for which of my
good parts did you first suffer love for me?
BENEDICK

Suffer love! a good epithet! I do suffer love
indeed, for I love thee against my will.
BEATRICE

In spite of your heart, I think; alas, poor heart!
If you spite it for my sake, I will spite it for
yours; for I will never love that which my friend hates.
BENEDICK

Thou and I are too wise to woo peaceably.
BEATRICE

It appears not in this confession: there's not one
wise man among twenty that will praise himself.
BENEDICK

An old, an old instance, Beatrice, that lived in
the lime of good neighbours. If a man do not erect
in this age his own tomb ere he dies, he shall live

no longer in monument than the bell rings and the
widow weeps.

BEATRICE

And how long is that, think you?

BENEDICK

Question: why, an hour in clamour and a quarter in
rheum: therefore is it most expedient for the
wise, if Don Worm, his conscience, find no
impediment to the contrary, to be the trumpet of his
own virtues, as I am to myself. So much for
praising myself, who, I myself will bear witness, is
praiseworthy: and now tell me, how doth your cousin?

BEATRICE

Very ill.

BENEDICK

And how do you?

BEATRICE

Very ill too.

BENEDICK

Serve God, love me and mend. There will I leave
you too, for here comes one in haste.

Enter URSULA

URSULA

Madam, you must come to your uncle. Yonder's old
coil at home: it is proved my Lady Hero hath been
falsely accused, the prince and Claudio mightily
abused; and Don John is the author of all, who is
fed and gone. Will you come presently?

BEATRICE

Will you go hear this news, signior?

BENEDICK

I will live in thy heart, die in thy lap, and be
buried in thy eyes; and moreover I will go with

thee to thy uncle's.

Exeunt

SCENE III.

A church.

Enter DON PEDRO, CLAUDIO, and three or four with tapers

CLAUDIO
Is this the monument of Leonato?
Lord
It is, my lord.
CLAUDIO
[Reading out of a scroll]
Done to death by slanderous tongues
Was the Hero that here lies:
Death, in guerdon of her wrongs,
Gives her fame which never dies.
So the life that died with shame
Lives in death with glorious fame.
Hang thou there upon the tomb,
Praising her when I am dumb.
Now, music, sound, and sing your solemn hymn.
SONG.
Pardon, goddess of the night,
Those that slew thy virgin knight;
For the which, with songs of woe,
Round about her tomb they go.
Midnight, assist our moan;
Help us to sigh and groan,
Heavily, heavily:
Graves, yawn and yield your dead,
Till death be uttered,

Heavily, heavily.

CLAUDIO

Now, unto thy bones good night!
Yearly will I do this rite.

DON PEDRO

Good morrow, masters; put your torches out:
The wolves have prey'd; and look, the gentle day,
Before the wheels of Phoebus, round about
Dapples the drowsy east with spots of grey.
Thanks to you all, and leave us: fare you well.

CLAUDIO

Good morrow, masters: each his several way.

DON PEDRO

Come, let us hence, and put on other weeds;
And then to Leonato's we will go.

CLAUDIO

And Hymen now with luckier issue speed's
Than this for whom we render'd up this woe.

Exeunt

SCENE IV.

A room in LEONATO'S house.

*Enter LEONATO, ANTONIO, BENEDICK, BEATRICE,
MARGARET, URSULA, FRIAR FRANCIS, and HERO*

FRIAR FRANCIS

Did I not tell you she was innocent?

LEONATO

So are the prince and Claudio, who accused her
Upon the error that you heard debated:
But Margaret was in some fault for this,
Although against her will, as it appears
In the true course of all the question.

114

ANTONIO
Well, I am glad that all things sort so well.
BENEDICK
And so am I, being else by faith enforced
To call young Claudio to a reckoning for it.
LEONATO
Well, daughter, and you gentle-women all,
Withdraw into a chamber by yourselves,
And when I send for you, come hither mask'd.

Exeunt Ladies

The prince and Claudio promised by this hour
To visit me. You know your office, brother:
You must be father to your brother's daughter
And give her to young Claudio.
ANTONIO
Which I will do with confirm'd countenance.
BENEDICK
Friar, I must entreat your pains, I think.
FRIAR FRANCIS
To do what, signior?
BENEDICK
To bind me, or undo me; one of them.
Signior Leonato, truth it is, good signior,
Your niece regards me with an eye of favour.
LEONATO
That eye my daughter lent her: 'tis most true.
BENEDICK
And I do with an eye of love requite her.
LEONATO
The sight whereof I think you had from me,
From Claudio and the prince: but what's your will?
BENEDICK
Your answer, sir, is enigmatical:

115

But, for my will, my will is your good will
May stand with ours, this day to be conjoin'd
In the state of honourable marriage:
In which, good friar, I shall desire your help.

LEONATO

My heart is with your liking.

FRIAR FRANCIS

And my help.
Here comes the prince and Claudio.

Enter DON PEDRO and CLAUDIO, and two or three others

DON PEDRO

Good morrow to this fair assembly.

LEONATO

Good morrow, prince; good morrow, Claudio:
We here attend you. Are you yet determined
To-day to marry with my brother's daughter?

CLAUDIO

I'll hold my mind, were she an Ethiope.

LEONATO

Call her forth, brother; here's the friar ready.

Exit ANTONIO

DON PEDRO

Good morrow, Benedick. Why, what's the matter,
That you have such a February face,
So full of frost, of storm and cloudiness?

CLAUDIO

I think he thinks upon the savage bull.
Tush, fear not, man; we'll tip thy horns with gold
And all Europa shall rejoice at thee,
As once Europa did at lusty Jove,
When he would play the noble beast in love.

BENEDICK

Bull Jove, sir, had an amiable low;
And some such strange bull leap'd your father's cow,
And got a calf in that same noble feat
Much like to you, for you have just his bleat.

CLAUDIO

For this I owe you: here comes other reckonings.

Re-enter ANTONIO, with the Ladies masked

Which is the lady I must seize upon?

ANTONIO

This same is she, and I do give you her.

CLAUDIO

Why, then she's mine. Sweet, let me see your face.

LEONATO

No, that you shall not, till you take her hand
Before this friar and swear to marry her.

CLAUDIO

Give me your hand: before this holy friar,
I am your husband, if you like of me.

HERO

And when I lived, I was your other wife:

Unmasking

And when you loved, you were my other husband.

CLAUDIO

Another Hero!

HERO

Nothing certainer:
One Hero died defiled, but I do live,
And surely as I live, I am a maid.

DON PEDRO

The former Hero! Hero that is dead!

LEONATO
She died, my lord, but whiles her slander lived.
FRIAR FRANCIS
All this amazement can I qualify:
When after that the holy rites are ended,
I'll tell you largely of fair Hero's death:
Meantime let wonder seem familiar,
And to the chapel let us presently.
BENEDICK
Soft and fair, friar. Which is Beatrice?
BEATRICE
[Unmasking] I answer to that name. What is your will?
BENEDICK
Do not you love me?
BEATRICE
Why, no; no more than reason.
BENEDICK
Why, then your uncle and the prince and Claudio
Have been deceived; they swore you did.
BEATRICE
Do not you love me?
BENEDICK
Troth, no; no more than reason.
BEATRICE
Why, then my cousin Margaret and Ursula
Are much deceived; for they did swear you did.
BENEDICK
They swore that you were almost sick for me.
BEATRICE
They swore that you were well-nigh dead for me.
BENEDICK
'Tis no such matter. Then you do not love me?
BEATRICE
No, truly, but in friendly recompense.

LEONATO

Come, cousin, I am sure you love the gentleman.

CLAUDIO

And I'll be sworn upon't that he loves her;
For here's a paper written in his hand,
A halting sonnet of his own pure brain,
Fashion'd to Beatrice.

HERO

And here's another
Writ in my cousin's hand, stolen from her pocket,
Containing her affection unto Benedick.

BENEDICK

A miracle! here's our own hands against our hearts.
Come, I will have thee; but, by this light, I take
thee for pity.

BEATRICE

I would not deny you; but, by this good day, I yield
upon great persuasion; and partly to save your life,
for I was told you were in a consumption.

BENEDICK

Peace! I will stop your mouth.

Kissing her

DON PEDRO

How dost thou, Benedick, the married man?

BENEDICK

I'll tell thee what, prince; a college of
wit-crackers cannot flout me out of my humour. Dost
thou think I care for a satire or an epigram? No:
if a man will be beaten with brains, a' shall wear
nothing handsome about him. In brief, since I do
purpose to marry, I will think nothing to any
purpose that the world can say against it; and
therefore never flout at me for what I have said

against it; for man is a giddy thing, and this is my
conclusion. For thy part, Claudio, I did think to
have beaten thee, but in that thou art like to be my
kinsman, live unbruised and love my cousin.

CLAUDIO

I had well hoped thou wouldst have denied Beatrice,
that I might have cudgelled thee out of thy single
life, to make thee a double-dealer; which, out of
question, thou wilt be, if my cousin do not look
exceedingly narrowly to thee.

BENEDICK

Come, come, we are friends: let's have a dance ere
we are married, that we may lighten our own hearts
and our wives' heels.

LEONATO

We'll have dancing afterward.

BENEDICK

First, of my word; therefore play, music. Prince,
thou art sad; get thee a wife, get thee a wife:
there is no staff more reverend than one tipped with
horn.

Enter a Messenger

Messenger

My lord, your brother John is ta'en in flight,
And brought with armed men back to Messina.

BENEDICK

Think not on him till to-morrow:
I'll devise thee brave punishments for him.
Strike up, pipers.

Dance

Exeunt

Biography

A Short Life of Edward de Vere, 17th Earl of Oxford

by Dr. Kevin Gilvary, President
The de Vere Society

He was born on 12 April 1550 at Castle Hedingham, his family's ancestral home. His father, John de Vere, 16th Earl, was Lord Great Chamberlain and attended the coronations of both Mary and Elizabeth Tudor. His mother was Margaret Golding. Edward was 11 when, in 1561, Queen Elizabeth visited Hedingham for four days of masques, feasting and entertainments. When his father died in 1562, young Oxford left to become, like Bertram in *All's Well that Ends Well*, a ward of the Crown under the guardianship of William Cecil, the Queen's private secretary (later Lord Burghley, Lord Treasurer). His mother married Charles Tyrrell and seems to have passed out of the boy's life. His sister Mary went to live with her stepfather and the siblings were not reunited for some years.

According to a curriculum in Cecil's own hand, Edward de Vere's daily studies included dancing, French, Latin, writing and drawing, cosmography, penmanship, riding, shooting, exercise and prayer. Edward de Vere showed a prodigious talent for scholarship from his early years, and we may ascribe his lifelong love of learning to the influence of two of his early tutors. The first was Sir Thomas Smith who was, perhaps, England's most respected Greek scholar and the former Cambridge tutor of Sir William Cecil. It was, no doubt, through Cecil's influence that Edward de Vere spent some time living in the household of Smith in his early years, during which time he spent about five months at Smith's alma mater, Queens' College, Cambridge. Smith was a scholar of widely varied interests – this was reflected in his 400-volume library, some of which is still extant at Cambridge. De Vere's other tutor was Laurence Nowell, who was not only an accomplished cartographer but was also England's premier scholar of Anglo-Saxon literature – it was Nowell who possessed the only known copy of *Beowulf*.

Another important influence on Edward de Vere's early studies was his maternal uncle Arthur Golding, an officer in the Court of Wards under Cecil, who is credited with the translation of Ovid's *Metamorphoses*, published in 1567, a book widely recognised as having a major influence on 'Shakespeare'.

Following on from his matriculation at Cambridge in November 1558, Edward was awarded an honorary MA by Cambridge during a Royal progress in August 1564, and another degree by Oxford University during a Royal progress in 1566. Edward de Vere then attended Gray's Inn to study law. One notable feature of the Elizabethan Inns of Court was a tradition of mounting dramatic productions and of hosting the various touring companies of players.

In 1570 he served in a military campaign in Scotland under the Earl of Sussex. By 1571, he was reported as a leading luminary of the Court and, for a time, a favourite of Queen Elizabeth. In December 1571 he married Anne Cecil, aged 15, daughter of his guardian. This was a dynastic marriage where all the advantage accrued to Cecil who, ennobled as Baron Burghley, had reduced the social gap between himself and the young Earl.

While Oxford was away on a Grand Tour of Europe, he heard that his daughter Elizabeth Vere had been born in July 1575. On his return in early 1576, he appeared to have been convinced that Elizabeth was not his child; consequently he became estranged from Anne for five years, and exiled himself from Court, taking up residence in the Savoy and concerning himself with literary and musical patronage.

Already, in 1573, *Cardanus Comfort* (the Consolations of Boethius) had been translated from Latin by Thomas Bedingfield and dedicated to Oxford; and published with a preface written by him. In 1576 an anthology, *A Paradise of Daintie Devices*, including several poems by Oxford, was published. These are juvenile works but already show affinities, in both style and thought, with those of the mature Shakespeare.

Oxford's Grand Tour had taken in Paris, Strasbourg, Venice, Genoa, Florence, Palermo and, on his way back through France, Rousillon – the setting for *Love's Labour's Lost*. Oxford spent the best part of a year travelling in Italy in 1576, and becoming involved with moneylenders. He came back to England fluent in Italian and well acquainted with the northern Italian cities, to be satirised by Gabriel Harvey as 'The Italian Earl'. On his way back his ship was attacked by pirates in the English Channel (cf. *Hamlet*). Fourteen of 'Shakespeare's' plays have Italian settings, in which he put his detailed knowledge of the country, beyond pure book knowledge, to good use.

1573 saw the birth of Henry Wriothesley, Earl of Southampton. Although history has not bequeathed to us any evidence of a direct relationship between the two men, in the relatively small world of the royal Court, they must have been acquainted with each other. The poems *Venus and Adonis* (1593) and *The Rape of Lucrece* (1594) were dedicated to Southampton. These were the first works to be published under the name 'Shakespeare' and for the next five years the records show the byline 'Shakespeare' to have been associated exclusively with these two poems. Plays under the name 'Shakespeare' did not appear in print until 1598, the year that Lord Burghley died.

In May 1577 Oxford invested in Frobisher's voyage in the ship *Edward Bonaventure*. Despite its name, the ship's voyage across the Atlantic in search of the North-West Passage lost money; consequently he was forced to sell three estates (cf. Hamlet's words 'I am but mad north-north-west' II.1.). In 1578 he invested in Frobisher's second expedition, which also lost money, forcing further sales of estates.

He was mentioned by Gabriel Harvey in an address to Queen Elizabeth in July 1578, as a prolific private poet and one 'whose countenance shakes spears'. In the same year John Lyly, Oxford's secretary, published *Euphues. The Anatomy of Wit*, followed in 1579 by *Euphues and his England*, dedicated to Oxford. These two books launched the fashion for 'Euphuism', a style characterized by high-flown language, satirized in *Love's Labour's Lost*.

In March 1581 Oxford's mistress, Anne Vavasour, who was one of Queen Elizabeth's Ladies of the Bedchamber, gave birth to a son. The lovers and their son were sent to the Tower by an infuriated Queen but swiftly released (cf. *Measure for Measure*). After his release, Oxford was wounded in a street-fight provoked by Thomas Knyvet, a kinsman of Anne Vavasour; affrays continued in the streets of London between the rival gangs of supporters for over a year (cf. *Romeo and Juliet*).

In December 1581 he resumed living with his long-suffering and devoted wife, and accepted Elizabeth

Vere as his child. Tragically, their only son died one day after his birth. Three more daughters followed, of whom Susan and Bridget survived.

In 1584, Robert Greene's *Gwydonius; the Card of Fancy* was dedicated to him, identifying him as a 'pre-eminent writer'. In 1586, when he was 36, he served on the tribunal which condemned Mary, Queen of Scots to execution.

In the same year, the Queen awarded Oxford an unconditional pension of £1,000 a year for life (about £500,000 at today's value). The motive for this uncharacteristic generosity on the part of the Queen remains a mystery – no accounting was required of Oxford. Her successor, King James I, continued to pay the pension. In reply to Sir Robert Cecil's request that Lord Sheffield's pension be increased, the King refused, saying, 'Great Oxford got no more . . .', leaving us to wonder why Great Oxford? His greatness does not seem to have resided in war or any of the known offices of State. Perhaps a clue can be found in a letter to Burghley, written in 1594, in which Edward de Vere seeks his favour in a matter involving what he describes as 'in mine office' and that this office is beholden to the Queen.

In 1589, George Puttenham published *The Arte of English Poesie* and this contains the most telling recognition of Edward de Vere's literary standing amongst his contemporaries: 'And in her Majesties time that now is are sprong up an other crew of Courtly makers Noble men and Gentlemen of her Majesties owne servantes, who have written excellently well as it would appeare if their doings could be found out and made publicke with the rest, of which number is first that noble Gentleman Edward Earle of Oxford.'

In 1588 his wife Anne, daughter of Lord Burghley, died and in extant letters written at this time, it is reported that Burghley is so incapacitated by grief over the death of his favourite daughter that he is incapable of conducting any Privy Council business.

Three years later, in 1591, Oxford married another of the Queen's Maids of Honour, Elizabeth Trentham, with whom he finally became the father of a male heir; Henry de Vere, 18th Earl of Oxford. Although there is evidence of his continued involvement in Court affairs, from the date of this marriage Edward de Vere's life at his new home at King's Place in Hackney is perhaps the most obscure of his entire life.

In 1594, his ship the *Edward Bonaventure* was wrecked in Bermuda (cf. *The Tempest*). In January 1595, Elizabeth Vere married William Stanley, 6th Earl of Derby, another literary earl who maintained his own company of players – many scholars believe that *A Midsummer Night's Dream* was written for these festivities which were attended by the whole royal Court.

On September 7 1598, Francis Meres' *Palladis Tamia* was registered for publication, naming Oxford as the 'best for comedy'. This is a vital document in Shakespearean history because it includes the first mention of 'Shakespeare' as a playwright, attributing twelve plays to him; until then Shakespeare's reputation had rested on the two narrative poems only.

Oxford suffered all his life from financial difficulties, much of which can be traced to the fact that Queen Elizabeth handed out the bulk of his estate to her favourite courtier the Earl of Leicester during Oxford's minority as a royal ward (estates which Oxford found almost impossible to reclaim), and the ruinous debt she placed upon him over his marriage to Anne Cecil. It is, however, notable that his new brother-in-law, the wealthy Staffordshire landowner and Knight of the Shire Francis Trentham, took over the management of Edward de

Vere's near-bankrupt estate from 1591 and gradually nursed it back to health so that, when Oxford died, all of his massive debts had been cleared.

On the Queen's death in 1603 Oxford wrote eloquently to Sir Robert Cecil, son and heir of Lord Burghley, of his 'great grief'. He wrote, 'In this common shipwreck, mine is above all the rest, who least regarded, though often comforted, she hath left to try my fortune among the alterations of time and chance'.

Oxford died in Hackney in 1604, cause unknown. Parish records state that he was buried in Hackney Church on July 6, but a family history by his first cousin Percival Golding, states 'Edward de Veer ... a man in mind and body absolutely accomplished with honorable endowments ... lieth buried at Westminster'. No record of such a burial can now be traced in Westminster Abbey, where there is a Vere family tomb.

The Aftermath of Oxford's life and death

During the winter season 1604-05, six of Shakespeare's plays were presented at Court by command of King James I. This has an air of commemoration. In 1609 the *Sonnets* were published in a pirated edition. The famous dedication describes the author as 'our ever-living', a phrase invariably used only of the dead.

In 1622 Henry Peacham published, in *The Compleat Gentelman*, a list of poets who made Elizabeth's reign a 'golden age'. Unaccountably, he omitted Shakespeare but placed the Earl of Oxford in first place in his list – perhaps he knew them to be the same person. This is unlike Meres who included them both – maybe one reason was because he didn't know Oxford and Shakespeare were the same person.

We do not know who instigated publication of the First Folio Edition of the Shakespeare plays in 1623, but there is no mention of any executor or relative of Shakspere of Stratford in connection with it. However, of the two brothers who financed it and to whom it was dedicated, one – Philip Earl of Montgomery – was the husband of Oxford's daughter Susan, while the other – William Earl of Pembroke – had once been a suitor for her sister Bridget. Pembroke was Lord Chamberlain, the supreme authority in the world of theatre, and thus in a position to decide which plays were to be published and which suppressed. We also know that Ben Jonson, who wrote much of the introductory material, was an intimate associate of the de Vere family after Oxford's death. The First Folio was therefore very much a family affair, but the family was not the one in Stratford-on-Avon.

An AfterVerse

For those with yet an interest
In strenuous debate
We've compiled a list of books and films
Your appetite to sate.
From this study clear your mind
Of doubt and all misgiving-
Who from us has long since gone
And who is ever-living.

Selected References & Bibliography
About the Author
Edward de Vere, 17th Earl of Oxford

Books

♦ Anderson, M. (2005). *Shakespeare by Another Name: The Life of Edward de Vere, Earl of Oxford, The Man who was Shakespeare.* New York: Gotham Books. *--A physicist by training with research interest in how evidence supports or negates a theory, Mark Anderson spent ten years investigating Edward de Vere as the author of Shake-speare's works.*

♦Farina, William. (2006). *De Vere as Shakespeare: An Oxfordian Reading of the Canon.* Jefferson, NC. McFarland & Company.

--Each of the plays and poems is individually assessed and explored in its own chapter, using the innumerable connections between the text itself and the life of its author, Edward de Vere.

♦ Looney, J. Thomas (2018). *Shakespeare Identified.* Cary, N.C. Veritas Publicaations.
--First published in 1920 this book began the modern Oxfordian movement. From reading it, Sigmund Freud became convinced and John Galsworthy called it "the best detective story I ever read."

♦ Ogburn, C. (1992). *The Mysterious William Shakespeare.* McLean (Va.): EPM.
--An in depth exploration and must read foundational book on the authorship question.

♦Sobran, Joseph. (1997). *Alias Shakespeare: Solving the Greatest Literary Mystery of All Time.*
New York; The Free Press, A Division of Simon & Schuster.
--A concise exploration of the puzzling questions surrounding the authorship controversy with the evidence decisively supporting the case for Edward de Vere, the 17th Earl of Oxford, as the rightful author of the Shakespeare plays and poems.

♦Whittemore, Hank. (2016), *100 Reasons Shake-speare Was the Earl of Oxford.*
Somerville MA. Forever Press.
► Also with further discussion and public comment at: *Hank Whittemore's Shakespeare Blog.*
        https://hankwhittemore.com/
--In both the book and online blog cited above, Whittemore presents a concise introduction to the

authorship question that examines 100 different aspects, from biographical and historical records, that point to Edward de Vere as the true writer of the Shake-speare plays and poems.

Websites & Videos

► De Vere Society. (2019). The de Vere Society – Dedicated to the proposition that the works of Shakespeare were written by Edward de Vere, 17th Earl of Oxford. [online] Deveresociety.co.uk. Available at: https://deveresociety.co.uk
--A very complete resource with substantial biographical and authorship information and links.

► The Oxford Fellowship (2019). Shakespeare Oxford Fellowship | Research and Discussion of the Shakespeare Authorship Question. [online] Shakespeare Oxford Fellowship. Available at: https://shakespeareoxfordfellowship.org/
--A seminal online resource especially focusing on the authorship question.

► Waugh, A. (2019). Alexander Waugh. [online] YouTube. Available at: https://www.youtube.com/channel/UCHN7SCKlsa9lPYJ mqqQ2uIg/featured/
OR simply search: 'Alexander Waugh'
--Alexander Waugh is a leading authorship scholar who has produced many fascinating video presentations on the authorship question. This link is to his YouTube Channel.

► Columbia Pictures & Centropolis Entertainment. (2011). *Anonymous.* Produced and directed by Roland Emmerich. [DVD]
--This mainstream film is both entertaining and enlightening. It presents a superb dramatization of the character of Edward de Vere, setting out in detail the historical and personal context which made his anonymous authorship necessary.

►Centropolis Entertainment and First Folio Pictures. *Last Will and Testament.* (2012). [DVD]
--A thoughtful and ground-breaking video documentary introduction to the Shakespeare authorship question.

Acknowledgment
Our sincere thanks to
The de Vere Society
and
The Shakespeare Oxford Fellowship
*for their inspiration, help and support
in creating this series.*

Attributions
*--Character list from Wikipedia under
the Creative Commons License 3.0
--Play text from the Moby(tm) editions
in the public domain*

Photos

Coat of Arms of Edward de Vere
Source: Wikimedia.org
Author: George Baker / Public domain

The Keep at Castle Hedingham
Source: geograph.org.uk
Author: David Phillips / CC BY-SA 2.0

The de Vere Family Coat of Arms
Source: Wikimedia
Author: Rs-nourse / CC BY-SA 3.0
(https://creativecommons.org/licenses/by-sa/3.0)

View from The Minstrels' Gallery, Hedingham Castle
Source: geograph.org.uk/p/3162585
Photo by: © PAUL FARMER - cc-by-sa/2.0

Cover/Inside: The Welbeck portrait of Edward de Vere (1575). Artist unknown. National Portrait Gallery, London.

This work has been edited and produced by

Verus Publishing
www.verusbooks.com

V | P

www.ingramcontent.com/pod-product-compliance
Lightning Source LLC
Chambersburg PA
CBHW030420100426
42812CB00028B/3037/J